FEB   2009

The Great Depression

Don Nardo

LUCENT BOOKS

A part of Gale, Cengage Learning

GALE
CENGAGE Learning

Detroit • New York • San Francisco • New Haven, Conn • Waterville, Maine • London

LIBRARY OF CONGRESS CATALOGING-IN-PUBLICATION DATA

Nardo, Don, 1947–
  The Great Depression / by Don Nardo.
    p. cm. — (American history)
  Includes bibliographical references and index.
  ISBN 978-1-4205-0033-2 (hardcover)
  1. Depressions—1929—United States—Juvenile literature. 2. United States--Economic conditions—1918-1945—Juvenile literature. 3. United States--Economic policy—1933–1945—Juvenile literature. 4. New Deal, 1933–1939—Juvenile literature. I. Title.
  HB37171929 .N25 2008
  330.973'0916—dc22

                                  2007037077

ISBN10: 1-4205-0033-3

Printed in the United States of America
2 3 4 5 6 7 12 11 10 09 08

Contents

Foreword

The United States has existed as a nation for just over 200 years. By comparison, Rome existed as a nation-state for more than 1,000 years. Out of a few struggling British colonies, the United States developed relatively quickly into a world power whose policy decisions and culture have great influence on the world stage. What events and aspirations drove this young American nation to such great heights in such a short period of time? The answer lies in a close study of its varied and unique history. As James Baldwin once remarked, "American history is longer, larger, more various, more beautiful, and more terrible than anything anyone has ever said about it."

The basic facts of United States history—names, dates, places, battles, treaties, speeches, and acts of Congress—fill countless textbooks. These facts, though essential to a thorough understanding of world events, are rarely compelling for students. More compelling are the stories in history, the experience of history.

Titles in this series explore history of a country and the experiences of Americans. What influences led the colonists to risk everything and break from Britain?

Who was the driving force behind the Constitution? Which factors led thousands of people to leave their homelands and settle in the United States? Questions like these do not have simple answers; by discussing them, however, we can view the past as a more real, interesting, and accessible place.

Students will find excellent tools for research and investigation in every title. Lucent Books' *American History* series provides not only facts, but also the analysis and context necessary for insightful critical thinking about history and about current events. Fully cited quotations from historical figures, eyewitnesses, letters, speeches, and writings bring vibrancy and authority to the text. Annotated bibliographies allow students to evaluate and locate sources for further investigation. Sidebars highlight important and interesting figures, events, or related primary source excerpts. Timelines, maps, and full-color images add another dimension of accessibility to the stories being told.

It has been said the past has a history of repeating itself, for good and ill. In these pages, students will learn a bit about both and, perhaps, better understand their own place in this world.

Important Dates at the Time

1928
October—During the national presidential campaign, Republican candidate Herbert Hoover insists that the federal government should play a minimal role in people's lives.

1929
October—The New York stock market crashes, sending the U.S. economy into a disastrous tailspin and starting the Great Depression.

1930
December—The once-powerful Bank of the United States, along with many other smaller banks, fails; 4.5 million Americans are now unemployed.

1920   1925   1930

1928
November—Hoover is elected president, defeating his Democratic opponent, Alfred E. Smith, by a wide margin.

1932
November—Running for president against Hoover, Franklin D. Roosevelt, governor of New York State, wins by a landslide.

1933
March—U.S. unemployment reaches a devastating 15 million; Roosevelt is inaugurated as the thirty-second president; he launches the massive legislative assault on the Depression, known thereafter as the New Deal.

1931
April—As the Great Depression tightens its grip on the American economy, automobile tycoon Henry Ford lays off 75,000 workers.

1932
January—President Hoover signs into law the Reconstruction Finance Corporation, designed to help put banks and large businesses back on their feet.

of the Great Depression

1933
May—Congress approves the Federal Emergency Relief Act, the Civilian Conservation Corps, the Tennessee Valley Authority, and other programs designed to fight the Depression.

1935
August—Roosevelt signs the Social Security Act, creating a national old-age pension system.

1937
April—The American economy finally reaches the level of output it had maintained in 1929 before the beginning of the Depression.

1939
War erupts in Europe as Germany, led by Nazi dictator, Adolf Hitler, invades Poland.

1935   1940   1945

1934
June—The Roosevelt administration launches the Indian Reorganization Act, which helps American Indians strengthen tribal governments.

1936
November—Roosevelt is reelected, defeating his Republican opponent, Kansas governor Alf Landon.

1938
June—Congress authorizes billions of dollars for new public works projects to fight the effects of the recent recession.

1936
February—The Supreme Court declares Roosevelt's Agricultural Adjustment Act unconstitutional.

1941–1945
The United States fights in World War II against Germany, Italy, and Japan; a virtual avalanche of American war production helps to pull the nation the rest of the way out of the Depression.

Trying to Imagine the Unimaginable

Large-scale disasters that adversely affect the lives of thousands of people occur on a fairly regular basis in the United States and around the globe. One of the worst examples in recent memory occurred in August 2005. Hurricane Katrina, the sixth strongest Atlantic hurricane ever recorded, struck the gulf coasts of Mississippi and Louisiana with titanic fury, causing widespread damage and misery. More than 1,800 people died, 3 million lost electrical power, and hundreds of thousands became unemployed and/or homeless. Even more recently, in May 2007, a gigantic tornado ripped through Greenberg, Kansas. Virtually the entire town was destroyed and nearly everyone lost their homes, their jobs, or both.

These, and similar disasters over the years, have one significant thing in common. Though devastating, they were localized events that affected only tiny portions of the country and society. If not for coverage in newspapers, television, radio, and other media, most Americans would not have noticed them. And though nearly everyone sympathized with the victims, few people outside the disaster areas could imagine what living in such dire conditions is like. That would require a catastrophe of national proportions that would plunge nearly all Americans into debilitating, even desperate, circumstances.

A national crisis of such epic proportions has occurred in the United States only once in the past 140 years. Called the Great Depression, it began in 1929 when the stock market crashed, and most of the millions of people who had invested in it lost their money. The effects of these losses immediately rippled outward, and, like a cancer, infected society at all levels. Thousands of banks failed, causing many people who had never even owned stocks to lose their life savings. And companies, stores, and other businesses laid off millions of workers, who were unable to find other jobs. With no way to make money, huge numbers of people were unable to pay their mortgages or rents and soon found themselves homeless.

What made the crisis particularly frightening and crippling was that it was not temporary. Today, when a disaster strikes, federal, state, and local agencies usually go to work quickly to aid the victims, providing shelter, food, and other necessities. In most cases, devastated local economies soon recover. But during the Great Depression, a massive failure of government occurred at all levels, in part because the collapse of prosperity was so immense that no one knew what to do to reverse it. As a result, as one historian puts it, "for more than ten long years the American people suffered an economic crisis unlike any they had ever known or anticipated."[1] It was not until the period of 1939–1942, as the Untied States geared up for an even greater crisis—entering World War II—that the country finally began to recover from its long national nightmare.

Living in Shacks

In fact, the United States did more than recover from the ravages of the Great Depression. The nation emerged from World War II as the mightiest and richest country in the world, and it has not relinquished that status in the more than six decades since. Several generations of Americans have known only economic opportunity and prosperity, and an ac-ceptable standard of living. With a few exceptions, moreover, even the nation's poorest citizens do not experience conditions nearly as desperate as those faced by a significant portion of the population in the 1930s.

For these reasons, it is often difficult for people today to grasp the true immensity and horrors of the Depression. Citing the numbers of people who lost their life savings and/or jobs is not enough. Mere statistics do not adequately convey the levels of hardship endured by individuals and families across the country. Indeed, after the passage of so many years, the only way that these past events can, in a sense, come back to life is through the personal memories and testimony of those who witnessed them first hand.

Take the example of housing conditions during the crisis. Millions of Americans, both in cities and rural areas, lived in small, flimsy shacks. After touring the Alabama countryside in 1937, two visitors described the humble dwelling of a father, mother, and four children:

> The cabin sits close to the ground, with a single layer of boards for a floor; one window, or rather window hole, in each room (no glass, a wooden shutter instead); a roof that leaks so badly that when the last baby was born [the mother's bed] had to be moved three times; walls without paper or plaster, of course—indeed, you can see daylight through their cracks.[2]

This shack is an example of the deplorable conditions that millions of Americans lived in during the Great Depression.

The shack had no electricity, no running water, and no toilets (forcing the residents to relieve themselves in a hole in the ground), all typical of poor rural America at the time. Yet at least the family had a roof over its head. At the height of the Depression, an Oklahoma woman, named Mary Owsley, reported:

> I knew one family there in Oklahoma City, a man and a woman, and seven children lived in a hole in the ground. . . . They had chairs and tables and beds back in that hole. And they had the dirt all braced up there, just like a cave.[3]

Not Enough Shoes and Food

Substandard housing was only one aspect of the crisis. Because of the widespread lack of jobs and money, many parents could not afford to buy themselves and their children decent clothes. "My children have got no shoes and clothing to go to school with," a West Virginia father stated in 1935, "and we haven't got enough bed clothes to keep us warm."[4] Food was also in short supply in cities and towns across the land. Various charities responded by setting up soup kitchens, where long lines of starving people formed every evening.

Peggy Terry, from Kentucky, later remembered:

> When we'd come home from school in the evening, my mother'd send us to the [local] soup line. [And] if you happened to be one of the first ones in line, you didn't get anything but water that was on top. So we'd ask the guy who was ladling out the soup . . . to please dip down to get some meat and potatoes from the bottom of the kettle.[5]

In 1932, a Philadelphia relief worker told some congressmen about some desperate food situations he had witnessed:

One woman borrowed 50 cents from a friend and bought stale bread for 3½ cents per loaf, and that is all they [her family] had for eleven days except for one or two meals. . . . One woman went along the docks and picked up vegetables that fell from the wagons. Sometimes the fish vendors gave her fish at the end of the day. On two different occasions, the family was without food for a day and a half.[6]

A man living in a tenement apartment in East Harlem, New York, described a similar plight, telling a government official:

Depression-era children eating a sparse meal consisting of potatoes and cabbage. Many Americans did not have enough to eat during the 1930s.

It is now seven months I am out of work. . . . I have four children who are in need of clothes and food. . . . My daughter who is eight is very ill and not recovering. My rent is [over]due two months and I am afraid of being put out [evicted].[7]

In fact, such threats of eviction was very real. In 1932 alone, approximately 230,000 American families were forced from their homes for nonpayment of rent. Many of these homeless people ended up sleeping in alleyways, parks, or even garbage dumps (where they huddled up near incinerators to keep warm).

"No Home, No Work, No Money"

Under such cruel conditions, and with no end or remedy in sight, it is perhaps not surprising that many people eventually became despondent and depressed. Some went so far as to take their own lives. Yet while these poor souls were in the minority, many others at least considered such drastic measures. One government relief worker reported in 1934 that almost every adult she had aided had "talked of suicide at one time or another."[8] In that same year, a Pennsylvania man asked a local government official:

Can you be so kind as to advise me as to which would be the most

humane way to dispose of myself and [my] family, as this is about the only thing that I see left to do. No home, no work, no money. We cannot go along this way.[9]

It is difficult for most modern Americans to imagine such levels of hardship and desperation. How did things get so bad in the United States that more than a few people slept in holes in the ground, and some parents considered killing their own children? Could a similar massive economic catastrophe strike the country in the future? To answer these questions, one must soberly examine how the Great Depression came about. One must also look at the manner in which the government responded to the crisis, both before and after the change from a Republican to a Democratic administration in 1933. Finally, it is imperative to consider how ordinary Americans adapted and survived, and how the nation's economy recovered. But it is crucial to realize that, though the Depression itself ended, its legacy did not. In the words of noted historian, Robert McElvaine:

No period in American history has more of importance to say to us now than does the Depression decade. Events in those years have determined the direction of our social and economic policies, our relationship to our government, and our political alignment ever since.[10]

Chapter One

The Onset of the Great Depression

The Great Depression began after the catastrophic crash of the stock market in New York in October 1929. However, the great market crash was not, by itself, the cause of the massive economic downturn that followed. Rather, it was the first major visible sign of that downturn, as well as a contributing factor among many others. The exact causes of the Depression are still debated by historians and economists, and may never be known for sure. But there is general agreement among experts that both the stock market crash and the Depression were mainly the result of a number of unsound economic and business trends and practices in the 1920s. The most likely scenario is that these worsened over time, and that their combined effects eventually precipitated the crash, which in turn hastened the onset of the Depression.

A significant part of the problem was that very few people in academic or government positions foresaw the coming of financial troubles. In fact, nearly everyone, from the president and his advisers, to professors of economics at universities, and to ordinary citizens, was surprised and shocked by the stock market crash. This was because the decade of the 1920s had seemed both prosperous and happy. True, large numbers of Americans—perhaps as many as 40 percent—were poor during the so-called Roaring Twenties, or the Jazz Age. Yet the rich got steadily richer, while the middle class—made up of families that earned between $2,000 and $5,000 a year—did well and grew larger. As noted American historian, Howard Zinn, describes it:

Unemployment was down, from 4,270,000 [people out of work] in 1921 to a little over 2 million in 1927. The general level of wages for workers rose. Some farmers made a lot of money. The 40 percent of all families who made over $2,000 a year could buy new gadgets: autos, radios, refrigerators. Millions of people were not doing badly—and they could shut out of the picture the others—the tenant farmers, black and white, [and] the immigrant families in the big cities either without work or not making enough to get the basic necessities.[11]

Thus, most people in the upper and middle classes focused on their own needs and wants, which were largely being met. They paid little or no attention to the marked division of the country's population into haves and have-nots, which turned out to be a serious mistake.

In a nutshell, wealth and prosperity were far too concentrated in society's topmost levels. There was, therefore, a very uneven distribution of wealth. Efforts by the haves to perpetuate this situation included unwise economic practices that ultimately proved disastrous.

Greed, Inequality, and Corruption

Just how big was this uneven distribution of wealth in the 1920s, and why did it pose a danger to economic stability? An important 1934 study by a well-known social policy research group, the Brookings Institution, found a stunning rift between rich and poor in pre-Depression America. In 1929, shortly before the stock market crash, a mere

A wealthy, American woman preparing to have tea in her garden. The uneven distribution of American wealth in the 1920s may be one of the causes of the Great Depression.

0.1 percent of American families held wealth and income equal to the entire bottom 42 percent of American families. As McElvaine explains:

Stated in absolute numbers, approximately 24,000 families had a combined income as large as that shared by more than 11.5 million poor and lower-middle-class families. Fully 71 percent of all American families . . . had incomes under $2,500. At the other extreme, the 24,000 richest families enjoyed annual incomes in excess of $100,000 and 513 American families reported incomes above $1 million [considered an enormous fortune at the time]. . . . [Moreover] nearly 80 percent of the nation's families—some 21.5 million households—had no savings whatsoever. The 24,000 families at the top—0.1 percent—held 34 percent of all savings.[12]

This meant that the greatest concentration of wealth in American history up to that time was held by a tiny handful of families. The danger that few economists and government officials foresaw was what might happen if many of these rich families suddenly lost their fortunes. These families largely controlled American industry and employed millions of ordinary wage earners. If their companies suddenly went under, those workers might lose their jobs. Furthermore, the stock prices of the failed big companies would plummet; and this might cause a panic in the stock market in which millions of ordinary investors could lose their money.

Meanwhile, hoping to get even richer, well-to-do investors increasingly engaged in risky business practices. Stock pools represented only one example. As the famed American historian, Samuel E. Morison, wrote:

A group of men would get together, buy a sizable block of stock of no matter what, then trade shares back and forth, hiking the price and pulling in outsiders who hoped to get in on the profits. When the stock reached an agreed point, members of the pool dumped it on the market [i.e., sold all their shares just before people learned that the stock was actually worth much less], took their profits, and retired, leaving the suckers to take the rap.[13]

Another risky financial venture that was common before the crash was investing in a holding company. Such a company did not make a product or provide a service. Rather, the operators of a holding company bought several other businesses and managed them, in return taking a percentage of the profit of each business. With occasional exceptions, a few wealthy individuals acquired and ran holding companies, in which hundreds of thousands of ordinary working people bought shares. The problem was that many of these managers were unscrupulous. They often mismanaged the companies while bleeding money from them to fill their own pockets.

Unwisely Trying to Eat the World

Although the stock market crash was a major factor in the onset of the Depression, many other factors contributed. Among them was a growing instability in trade relations between the United States and other nations, as explained by historian, Robert McElvaine.

By the late twenties, each country was seeking to advance its own interests, even if in the process it worsened the positions of others. In a delicate, interdependent world economy, these "beggar thy neighbor" tactics were suicidal. Nowhere should this have been more clear than in the Untied States. This country was trying nothing less in the 1920s than to be the world's banker, food producer, and manufacturer, but to buy as little as possible from the world in return. This attempt to eat the world and have it, too, was the epitome of a self-defeating policy [and] . . . If the United States would not buy from other countries, there was no way for others to buy from Americans, or to meet interest payments on American loans. The weakness of the international economy and [unwise] American foreign policy unquestionably contributed to the coming of the Great Depression.

Robert McElvaine, *The Great Depression: America 1929–1941*. New York: Random House, 1993, pp. 34–35.

Such companies had a high risk of failure, therefore, and when they went out of business they left the ordinary investors with worthless shares. As such flimsy companies increased in number, the risk of damage to tens of thousands of investors and to the national economy as a whole also increased.

A Loaded Gun

These, and other financial inequities and shady business practices, were not the only contributors to the market crash and the Depression. Several other factors involved the mass production of goods, consumer spending, and consumer borrowing and its effects on banks. For example, most of the larger American farms significantly increased their levels of production in the 1920s. In fact, thinking that the economy would continue to expand, these well-off farmers overproduced to a great extent; in doing so they created a large surplus of crops and other farm products. This had the unintended effect of causing the prices of these products to drop. In turn, small farmers found it more difficult to make a profit, and faced an increased risk of going under if the economy suddenly slumped.

Similarly, many manufacturing industries produced more goods than average Americans could afford to buy. As a result, in 1928 and 1929, not long before the market crash, these companies began cutting back on production. This inevitably meant laying off some of their workers. In turn, the people who lost their jobs stopped buying many products, increasing the surplus of those goods, and thereby causing still more cutbacks in production and job losses.

Banks were adversely affected, too, partly because jobless people dipped into their savings, decreasing the amount of money banks had to invest. But even more ominous for banks was the worsening situation with credit and debt. Many struggling small farmers took out business loans, and millions of ordinary consumers bought all manner of goods on credit. By 1929, 60 percent of all cars and 80 percent of all radios were purchased on credit. Between 1925 and 1929, the amount owed to banks by borrowers more than doubled, from $1.4 billion to $3 billion. Because increasingly large numbers of people found themselves unable to pay their debts, many

banks teetered on the brink of collapse or even had to close their doors.

In short, though good times seemed to reign in the 1920s, numerous serious instabilities lurked beneath the surface of the country's economic bubble. Eventually, their combined effects made collapse likely, if not inevitable. Noted journalist, Edward R. Ellis, who lived through the Depression, memorably summed up the situation:

> Greedy people wanted more than they needed. Foolish people thought they could get something for nothing. Impulsive people bought now in the hope of paying later. Income and wealth were distributed unfairly and dangerously. . . . The masses were not paid enough money to consume all the goods they produced. . . . The corporate structure was sick. The banking system was weak. . . . This constellation of conditions left the economy a flawed and loaded gun,

By 1929, sixty percent of cars, like this 1927 Lincoln Phaeton, were purchased on credit. Some banks had to shut down during the Depression because Americans were unable to pay such debts.

and when the stock market crashed, the gun did not merely fire—it exploded in everyone's face.[14]

The Bubble Bursts

The great crash did not happen all in one day. Rather, the New York Stock Exchange suffered a series of devastating blows over the course of a little more than a week, beginning in the afternoon of October 21, 1929. At that time, the market suddenly slumped when thousands of investors, worried that their stocks were declining in worth, sold them. As more and more people dumped their stocks, a general panic set in, producing the heaviest selling binge on record.

Hysteria on Wall Street

American historian, James D. Horan, gives this brief but vivid account of the 1929 stock market crash.

On the afternoon of October 24, 1929, the first hammer-blow smashed down on [the] arrogantly self-comfortable world. A total of 12,894,650 shares swamped the board and rocked the financial district. Hysteria swept through Wall Street like a wind-fanned prairie fire. Brokers collapsed under the strain of trying to keep up with orders to sell. . . . The plunge had carried down with it speculators, big and little, in every part of the country, wiping out thousands of accounts. . . . Five days later, on October 29—Black Tuesday—Wall Street

The front page of the Brooklyn Daily Eagle *reporting the Stock Market crash on October 29, 1929.*

was in a real panic. The stock market had collapsed. Sixteen million shares were tossed overboard on the New York Stock Exchange for whatever price could be obtained. . . . [In modern dollars] the loss was the equivalent of 250 to 500 billion dollars. But the damage to confidence was even more costly. The economic life of the country was smothered in gloom.

James D. Horan, *The Desperate Years.* New York: Bonanza, 1962, pp. 10–11.

A crowd gathers on Wall Street in New York City after hearing about the Stock Market crash.

In fact, the stock sales were so intense that by the end of the day the ticker machine, used to record transactions, was running a hundred minutes behind the actual sales.

Ben Isaacs, a Chicago man who sold clothes on credit to lower-middle-class people, later remembered the commotion: "I was going on my business [calls] and I heard the newspaper boys calling, running all around the streets and [saying] 'Stock market crashed! Stock market crashed!' [The news] came out just like lightning."[15]

The market panic continued in the days that followed. On Monday, October 28, the stock market lost an unprecedented $14 billion. And the very next day, the market took another huge hit, losing $15 billion and bringing the losses for that disastrous nine-day period to an incredible $50 billion. That is the equivalent of many hundreds of billions of dollars in today's money. The people immediately affected for the worse, of course, were mainly rich or middle-class individuals who could afford to play the market. A number of them were so distraught over their losses that they took their own lives. Arthur A. Robinson, then a wealthy businessman, later recalled what happened to a successful cigar company:

> The market collapsed. I got a call from the company president. Could I loan him $200 million? I refused, because at the time I had to protect my own [business]. His $115 stock dropped to $2 and he jumped out of the window of his Wall Street office.[16]

Another well-to-do observer who managed to survive the crash intact—Sidney J. Weinberg, said:

I don't know anybody that jumped out of the window. But I know many who threatened to jump. They ended up in nursing homes and insane asylums and things like that. These were people who were trading in the market or in banking houses. They broke down physically as well as financially.[17]

As the days wore on, the rich were not the only ones who experienced shock and despair. The effects of the enormous losses in the stock market rapidly rippled outward, engulfing most of the rest of society, as historian, Gerald W. Johnson, explains:

When the panic of 1929 suddenly wiped out the whole value of many stocks and sharply reduced the values of others, a great number of people who had thought themselves . . . at least well-off, found themselves with much less than they had thought they had, or with nothing at all. By [the] millions they quit buying anything except what they had to have to stay alive. This drop in spending threw the stores into trouble, and they quit ordering [new products] and discharged clerks. When orders stopped, the factories shut down, and factory workers had no jobs.[18]

This destructive financial chain reaction forced the national economy to begin a debilitating downward spiral. As consumer buying significantly slowed, many people who were uncomfortable about keeping their money in banks withdrew these funds and hid them under their mattresses or in their attics. They also defaulted, or failed to make payments, on their bank loans. Both of these practices fatally wounded hundreds of banks, which had to close down. When this occurred, those customers who had not yet withdrawn their savings lost them, suddenly thrusting them into poverty.

Meanwhile, some of these unfortunate folks, along with many others, lost their jobs as businesses, both big and small, laid off large portions of their workforces. Unemployment rates, which had stood at about 3 percent before October 1929, rose to 9 percent by early in 1930. In the next two years the rise continued and reached a crippling 25 percent. This was a devastating situation because unemployment insurance and social security, which today help temporarily jobless people survive, did not exist at the time.

"Can You Spare a Dime?"

Ben Isaacs's business was among those that suffered because many of his customers who owed him money could not afford to pay him. As he later recalled:

We lost everything. [Normally] I would collect four [or] five hundred dollars a week [from my customers]. After [the crash], I couldn't collect fifteen [or even] ten dollars a week. I was going around trying to collect enough money to keep my

Please Buy My Apples

Beginning early in 1930, with the American economy continuing to slide downward, one of the more familiar symbols of the Depression appeared—the apple peddler. People from all walks of life set up little wooden carts or stands on street corners in both cities and towns. They sold their apples for from 2 to 5 cents each. Pathetically, some of the men who did so had not long before been well-paid businessmen, engineers, and stock brokers. There was typically a sign above the cart reading: "Please Buy an Apple," or "Help the Unemployed," or "Apples for Sale." In New York City, male and female apple peddlers acquired their produce by lining up before dawn outside the Apple Grower's Association at West and Harrison streets on the east side of Manhattan. Sadly, when there were apple shortages, some of these desperate folks went away empty handed.

Two unemployed people selling apples in New York City. The apple peddler became one of the most familiar symbols of the Depression.

family going. It was impossible. . . . We tried to struggle along, living day by day. Then I couldn't pay the rent. I had a little car . . . [and] I sold it for $15 in order to buy some food for the family.[19]

Eventually, Isaacs had to go on relief—that is, accept handouts of money, food, and clothing from charities. But even that did not halt his family's downward slide:

I went on relief and they gave me $45 a month. . . . So how [far] can that $45 go? I was paying $30 on the rent. I [had to] find another, cheaper [apartment, heated by a] stove, for $15 a month. I'm telling you, today a dog wouldn't live in that type of a place. Such a dirty, filthy, dark place. . . . About two months later, all of a sudden—no water. The city closed [down the building's water supply] for the [landlord's] nonpayment of the water bill. My wife used to carry two pales of water from [a neighboring building] and bring it up for us to wash the kids and to flush the toilet with it.[20]

In another big American city hit hard by the Depression's onset—New York— hundreds of thousands of citizens lived in the same degrading conditions that Ben Isaacs's family did in Chicago. Struggling songwriter, Yip Harburg, witnessed the worsening plight of many of these down-and-out people. He later told noted Depression historian, Studs Terkel:

I was walking along the street and you'd see the breadlines [in which] fellows with burlap on their shoes were lined up all along Columbus Circle, and went for blocks and blocks around the park, waiting. . . . The prevailing greeting at that time, on every block you passed, by some poor guy coming up, was: "Can you spare a dime?" Or: "Can you spare something for a cup of coffee?" . . . "Brother, Can You Spare a Dime?" finally hit on every block, on every street.[21]

Harburg soon transformed that sad plea for spare change into what became a sort of Great Depression anthem recognized by everyone.

People everywhere naturally wondered when the crisis would end, when life would get back to normal, and when people would regain their jobs, security, and dignity. In May 1930, some seven months after the onset of the Depression, President Herbert Hoover tried to raise people's spirits. "We have now passed the worst,"[22] he declared with considerable confidence. At the time, no one could imagine just how wrong this forecast would turn out to be.

Chapter Two

Hoover's Inadequate Remedies

F ew American presidents have had a legacy as poor as that of Herbert Hoover (1874–1964) or have been criticized and reviled as much as he has. This is partly because he had the unenviable distinction of occupying the White House when the stock market crashed and the Great Depression began. But most of all, Hoover has been faulted for the ways he handled the crisis. At least at first, critics say, he did not recognize how bad it really was; and in the long run, his administration's legislative and economic attempts to alleviate it were stunningly ineffective.

There is no doubt that Hoover and his chief advisers were far too shortsighted about the severity of the economic downturn. They believed it was only temporary, and that it would largely reverse itself through ordinary market forces, which they saw as ultimately sound and self-healing. "Any lack of confidence in the basic strength of [Ameri-

can] business," Hoover declared, less than a month after the market crash, "is foolish." Fewer than three months later, on January 21, 1930, the president announced, "Business and industry have turned a corner." Equally naive and deceptive was a statement made by his secretary of labor, James J. Davis, in June 1930. As prices of crops and other staple commodities were dropping to dangerously low levels, Davis optimistically reported: "Courage and resource are already swinging us back on the road to recovery. And we are fortunate in having a president who sets us a shining example of that courage and initiative."[23]

With such unrealistic attitudes about the growing national crisis, it is not surprising that the response of Hoover's government was, in general, inadequate. Much of the problem was the overly conservative attitude of top administration officials. In their view, it would be inappropriate and unwise for the federal

Red Cross workers give out boxes of seeds during the Depression. President Herbert Hoover relied on private charities and local relief efforts to provide aid to those in need.

government to provide massive free aid, which they saw as nothing less than government charity. Rather, they held, the best way to reverse the economic downturn was to rely on the strength of Americans to help themselves, aided by private charities and local relief efforts. This constituted "the very ethos of a white, Protestant culture, the image that Hoover and his kind held up as the ideal of Americanism," historian T.H. Watkins points out:

Hard work, honesty, and independence, they believed utterly, had brought this country to the forefront of nations, had built a breed of men (and women, too, some conceded, though not often) who had taken the institutions of the founding fathers and made them the wonder of the world. Anything that might weaken the strength of that tradition would weaken the very character of America and was, by definition, evil. Government charity, especially, by robbing people of initiative, would be the very embodiment of error. The national government should stay out of the personal lives of its citizens, even if they were in trouble.[24]

This reliance on self-initiative, self-help, and existing charities did not work, however. In fact, it only made things worse. In May and June 1930, the stock market suffered more serious declines as sales of automobiles and other popular commodities dropped well below their 1928 levels. As a result, the Depression's solid grip on the economy and society tightened, throwing more and more people out of work and into poverty.

Self-Help and Rugged Individualism

It must be emphasized that Hoover was neither an incompetent politician nor an insensitive individual. He was both caring and hard-working. And all available evidence indicates that he sincerely believed that his approach to restoring the nation's economic health was the correct one. The problem lies mostly with the economic philosophy he and his supporters advocated. It was founded on the ideas of hard work, free enterprise unhindered by government, and meeting

Self-Help the Answer to Poverty

Hoover was not the only wealthy, powerful American to say that the Depression's ills could be cured by simple self-help and self-reliance. The famous auto manufacturer, Henry Ford, advocated this same philosophy in a journal editorial published in June 1932, suggesting that all struggling people could support themselves by growing their own food.

Methods of self-help are numerous and great numbers of people have made the stimulating discovery that they need not depend on employers to find work for them—they can find work for themselves. . . . The land! That is where our roots are [and] from the land comes everything that supports life. . . . The land has not collapsed or shrunk in either extent or productivity. It is there waiting to honor all the labor we are willing to invest in it. . . . Let every man and every family in this season of the year cultivate a plot of land and raise a sufficient supply for themselves and others. Every city and village has vacant space whose use would be permitted.

Henry Ford, "On Unemployment," *Literary Digest,* June 11, 1932.

Before becoming president, Herbert Hoover was in charge of U.S. food programs during World War I, in which he helped to feed millions of Europeans.

the needs of society's have-nots through charitable organizations.

Hoover's entire life before becoming president had been shaped by these and similar ideas. After graduating from Stanford University in 1895 with a geology degree, he became a successful mining engineer. After making his fortune, he began devoting much of his time to relief work for people in need. He was particularly active in programs that fed homeless, starving Europeans during World War I, and, in 1917, President Woodrow Wilson put him in charge of U.S. food programs in the war effort. Hoover was so even-handed that he supplied aid to millions of starving Rus-

sians in the aftermath of the Communist takeover in Russia. Roundly criticized for aiding communism, he resolutely replied: "Twenty million people are starving. Whatever their politics, they shall be fed!"[25]

Having made a name for himself as a humanitarian, in the early 1920s Hoover served as secretary of commerce under President Warren G. Harding. In this post, Hoover worked to forge voluntary partnerships between government, big businesses, and major charities. He was praised for coordinating relief efforts after disastrous floods ravaged the Mississippi valley in 1927. The following year, he ran for president, often saying in his stump speeches, "We in America today are nearer to the final triumph over poverty than ever before in the history of any land."[26]

These words now sound hollow considering that barely a year later the stock market collapsed and millions of people became poverty-stricken. Yet when Hoover uttered them, he deeply believed that individuals, through personal ambition and hard work, could and would make poverty a thing of the past. He explained that philosophy in his now famous "rugged individualism" speech, delivered in October 1928, shortly before the presidential election. America's social system, he said:

> is founded upon the conception that only through ordered liberty, freedom, and equal opportunity to the individual will his initiative and enterprise spur on the march of progress. And in our insistence upon equality of opportunity has our system advanced beyond all the world.[27]

"Our system" worked so well, Hoover held, because the central government played as minimal a role as possible in business. This left business owners and managers to hire and fire, manufacture and market goods, and invest well-earned capital (money). Such an approach, he said, was only right for an independent, self-governing nation. In contrast, "When the federal government undertakes to go into commercial business," Hoover warned, "it immediately finds itself in a labyrinth [maze], every

alley of which leads to the destruction of self-government." When big government tries to create and control industry and business, he stated, it robs individuals of the right to do so on their own. It also dangerously increases governmental power, potentially threatening people's liberty. "The departure from our American system," Hoover declared, "will jeopardize the very liberty and freedom of our people."[28] Even after the initial onset of the Depression, the new president refused to waver from this basic philosophy of self-help and fear of big government intervention. In a February 1931 press statement, he said:

> This is not an issue as to whether people shall go hungry or cold in the United States. It is solely a question of the best method by which hunger and cold shall be prevented. It is a question of whether the American people . . . will maintain the spirit of charity and mutual self help [as opposed to] appropriations out of the Federal Treasury for such purposes. . . . If we break down this sense of responsibility and individual generosity . . . [it will impair] something infinitely valuable in the life of the American people. . . . I am confident that our people have the resources, the initiative, the courage, the stamina, and the kindliness of spirit to meet this situation in the way they have met their problems over generations.[29]

Opposed to Federal Unemployment Relief

In a May 1931 report, the U.S. Chamber of Commerce agreed with President Hoover that providing relief through federal unemployment insurance was a bad idea.

Unemployment is not, from an insurance point of view, a practical field for governmental intervention. Government compulsory insurance where it has so far been tried, in Europe, has proved inadequate through lack of sufficient reserves and has inevitably led to outright government payments, as in the English dole [welfare system]. It has thus [caused] and encouraged unemployment. Needed relief should be provided through private contributions and by state and local governments. There is every evidence that all requirements can in this manner be adequately met. Any proposals for federal appropriations for such purposes should therefore be opposed.

Quoted in William Dudley, ed., *The Great Depression: Opposing Viewpoints*. San Diego: Greenhaven Press, 1994, p. 28.

Hoover's Initiatives

Despite Hoover's very conservative philosophy of government and economic affairs, he did not think that his administration had no role to play in alleviating the crisis. He simply felt that the government should do only those things that were appropriate for it to do. Years before, to help European refugees and American flood victims, he had organized and coordinated relief efforts by businesses, charities, and government agencies. And faced with the economic downturn that followed the crash of 1929, he employed the same approach. Late that year, the president summoned leading industrialists and government officials to the White House. He persuaded most of them, including the wealthy car manufacturer, Henry Ford, to agree not to cut wages for those workers who still had jobs. Hoover also convinced the heads of the big utility companies to spend more on new construction programs. The hope was that this would create some needed jobs.

In addition, Hoover devoted considerable time and energy to organizing charity drives. During the winter of 1929–1930, he made numerous appeals to wealthy Americans, big companies, and churches, asking them to donate money and goods to the poor. But this effort produced only $15 million, a measly amount considering the scope of the national crisis. Some congressmen urged the president to launch government-funded relief efforts. But he refused.

Hoover also declined proposals that the government create a big public works program to put people back to work. He called it "the most gigantic pork-barrel [project] ever perpetrated by the American Congress."[30]

Hoover and his advisers believed that another way they could aid the ailing economy was by lowering tariffs. These are the duties, or taxes, that foreign countries and companies pay to the United States for the privilege of selling it products. The president reasoned, probably rightly, that lowering U.S. tariffs would encourage foreigners to lower their own tariffs; that would stimulate more international desire for U.S. products and spur new production and job creation at home. However, Congress took an opposite, more paranoid, and ultimately wrong-headed approach. In June 1930, legislators passed the Hawley–Smoot Tariff Act.

Designed to encourage production and use of U.S.-made products at home, it imposed a tariff of 60 percent or more

Workers building cars at the Ford Motor Company factory in Dearborn, Michigan. During the Depression President Hoover persuaded Henry Ford not to cut the wages of workers who he still employed.

on some 3,200 imported products, quadrupling former import duties. Some one thousand economists saw the danger that Hawley–Smoot posed, and signed a petition urging Hoover not to sign the bill. But Republican lawmakers lobbied him hard, and he reluctantly signed it. The results, as the economists had predicted, were disastrous, as many foreign nations retaliated by raising their own tariffs. Between 1930 and 1933, imports fell by two-thirds and exports fell from $5.4 billion to $1.4 billion.

Still another Hoover initiative that backfired was the Revenue Act of 1932. It was a huge tax increase, mostly in the form of sales taxes, meant to raise needed money for the new federal programs. People with the highest incomes saw their taxes rise from 25 percent to 63 percent, while the estate tax doubled, and a 2-cent tax was imposed on all bank checks. Opposition to the Revenue Act was widespread throughout the country.

One of the federal programs that the Revenue Act helped fund was the Reconstruction Finance Corporation (RFC), created early in 1932. An earnest, though far too modest, effort to halt the economic downslide, the RFC loaned money to failing banks, railroads, insurance companies, and other big businesses. The intention was to ensure that these institutions remained intact and solvent. That would hopefully create jobs, or at least maintain existing ones, and thereby help the economy. "I want to break the ice by lending to industry so that somebody will begin to spend in a big way,"[31] said Hoover's treasury secretary, Ogden Mills. The RFC did save many businesses, and was also helpful when it began loaning money to individual states late in 1932. But it was not enough by itself to significantly loosen the Depression's stranglehold on the economy.

A Financial Pit

In fact, the combined efforts of the Hoover administration to fight the Depression failed. Month by month, year by year, the country sank deeper and deeper into a financial pit. Between November 1929 and January 1933, more than 9,000 U.S. banks failed and closed their doors. About 4,000 of these, with combined deposits of $3.6 billion, shut down in the first two months of 1933 alone. Because depositors had no insurance to back up their money, millions of Americans lost their entire life savings in a fleeting, tragic instant.

U.S. business and manufacturing losses during Hoover's term were also staggering. More than 26,000 businesses failed in 1930, and more than 28,000 went under the following year. Late in 1931, the nation's volume of manufacturing was only 54 percent of what it had been before the 1929 market crash. The plight of a single big corporation, the Pullman Car and Manufacturing Company, is illustrative of the overall trend. Late in 1933, its main factory could afford to employ only about 800 people, compared to some 8,000 before the crash. Pullman also had to reduce the number of its rail-

In 1930, more than 26,000 U.S. businesses, like this coffee shop, were forced to close.

road porters from 12,000 to 8,000 and its train conductors from 2,400 to 1,600. Tradesmen suffered even worse. Chicago officials reported that of the city's 125,000 carpenters, painters, plumbers, and other tradesmen, only about 10,000 worked regularly in the last two years of the Hoover presidency. The rest barely paid their rents by doing occasional odd jobs, or could no longer make ends meet and became homeless.

Indeed, huge numbers of families became homeless during Hoover's years in office. Because so many people blamed Hoover's administration for the crisis, or at least for its failure to halt it, shantytowns and other enclaves of homeless people became known as "Hoovervilles." In 1932, the journalist, Charles Walker, discovered such a place at the town dump in Youngstown, Ohio. "The inhabitants," he told his readers:

> were not, as one might expect, outcasts or 'untouchables,' or even hoboes. . . . They were men without

The Horrors of Hooverville

In 1932, journalist Charles Walker told his readers about a shantytown he found at the town dump in Youngstown, Ohio.

Back of the garbage house, there are at least three acres of waste land, humpy with ash heaps and junk. . . . When you come close, there is no doubt but that the dump is inhabited. [It is] a collection of shanty hamlets [and] from 150 to 200 men live in the shanties. The place is called by its inhabitants—Hooverville. I went forward and talked to the men. They showed me their houses. These vary greatly from mere caves covered with a piece of tin, to weather-proof shanties built of packing boxes. . . . Most of the men cook in communal fashion over a fire shielded by bricks in the open. . . . This pitiable village would be of little significance if it existed only in Youngstown, but nearly every town in the United States has its shantytown for the unemployed, and the same instinct has named them all "Hooverville."

Men standing around a shantytown, or Hooverville, during the Depression.

Quoted in William E. Leuchtenburg, ed., *The New Deal: A Documentary History*. New York: Harper and Row, 1968, p. 11.

jobs. Life [for them] is sustained by begging, eating at the city soup kitchens, or earning a quarter by polishing an automobile.[32]

Blood in the Streets

Motivated by the worsening economic conditions in the country, some people staged public demonstrations to show the government their anger and frustra-tion. Thousands of such marches and rallies took place across the country during the Hoover years. What the government tried to keep quiet then, and is still ignored in many history books, is that police and other officials often used violent means to break up these protests. In July 1931, for instance, five hundred unemployed men who gathered on a Detroit street were roughly dispersed by police. And the following month in

Indiana Harbor, Indiana, police used clubs to break up 1,500 jobless men who had gone to a local employer to demand jobs.

The most notorious use of government force to quell public discontent over the worsening Depression took place in the nation's capital. During the summer of 1932, some 20,000 World War I veterans marched in Washington, D.C., to demand that the government give them bonus money that they had been promised but had never received. These men camped out near the Capitol in tents and makeshift shelters, waiting for Congress or the president to act. This so-called "Bonus Army" soon had to deal with the real army. Four cavalry units, four infantry companies, a machine gun unit, and six tanks converged on the demonstrators. Unprovoked, the soldiers attacked the veterans with tear gas, then set fire to their shelters. More than a thousand demonstrators were badly injured by the gas. And in the huge scuffle that ensued, two veterans and a baby belonging to another were killed.

These over-zealous government reactions to legitimate dissent only deepened the ugly national mood and widening

The U.S. military burning the shacks built by the Bonus Army in Washington, D.C., in 1932. During the scuffle between the military and the Bonus Army more than 1,000 people were injured.

public opinion that Hoover and his administration had to go. In retrospect, it is clear that the president did not cause the Depression. But in spite of his good intentions, a bad situation grew worse on his watch. And rightly or wrongly, most people ended up blaming him for the evils of the crisis. One woman angrily declared:

> People are starving because of Herbert Hoover. My mother was out of work because of [him]. Men were killing themselves because of [him], and their fatherless children were being packed away to orphanages.[33]

Indeed, no single American in living memory seemed to have fallen so far from grace as Hoover had. Emblematic was the case of a Republican couple, who, in 1928, had proudly named their baby son, Herbert Hoover Jones. Four years later, the disappointed and furious parents went to court and had the child officially renamed Franklin D. Roosevelt Jones. The boy's new namesake, a Democrat, had just been elected president on promises that he would end the country's economic nightmare. Hopes for a new beginning were high across the land. But beneath the surface lurked a natural and understandable question: Could the new president deliver on these promises?

Chapter Three

Roosevelt and the Hundred Days

By the summer of 1932, a few months prior to that year's presidential election, the United States, along with many other nations, was trapped in the depths of the worst economic slump in modern history. Tens of millions of Americans were unemployed and living in poverty. Moreover, there was little hope that the situation would improve any time soon, for the federal government had clearly failed to alleviate the crisis. Overall, the U.S. national mood was fearful, perplexed, miserable, and angry. Most of the anger was directed toward the Republican Hoover administration. And there were growing sentiments among people of all ages, professions, and political persuasions that the country needed to bring in new management—to give the Democrats a shot at turning things around.

Fully aware that they had a real opportunity to seize the White House, the Democrats were optimistic about the coming election. At their national convention, held in Chicago in late June and early July, they nominated the governor of New York, Franklin Delano Roosevelt (1882–1945), as their presidential candidate. On July 2, he addressed the convention, giving what turned out to be a historic speech. Aiming his words not just at fellow Democrats, but at all Americans, he began to outline a possible new path to recovery. The speech also introduced to the nation, the world, and history the term that would ever after describe his fierce attack on the Depression—the "New Deal":

My program is based upon this simple moral principle. The welfare and the soundness of a nation depends first upon what the great mass of the people wish and need; and second, whether or not they are getting it. What do the people of America want more than anything

Delegates at the 1932 Democratic National Convention celebrate the nomination of Franklin D. Roosevelt as the candidate for president.

else? To my mind, they want two things: work, with all the moral and spiritual values that go with it; and with work, a reasonable measure of security, security for themselves and for their wives and children. . . . I pledge you, I pledge myself, to a new deal for the American people.

Let us all here assembled constitute ourselves prophets of a new order of competence and of courage. This is more than a political campaign; it is a call to arms. Give me your help, not to win votes alone, but to win in this crusade to restore America to its own people.[34]

The American people heard Roosevelt's call to arms loud and clear, and elected him president in a landslide. He wasted no time in initiating several of many New Deal programs designed to attack the Depression and put the country back on its feet. Indeed, the first three months of the new president's tenure in office proved historic for the sheer scope and audacity of that attack. Those months, now commonly called the "Hundred Days," witnessed the single-most ambitious and constructive spurt of presidential-congressional activity in American history. Employing a potent mixture of political power and personal moral authority, Roosevelt bent the legislature to his will.

Congress became almost literally his rubber stamp as he submitted and saw passed into law one sweeping legislative bill after another. Never before or since did a U.S. president hold such commanding authority or enjoy the backing of so many diverse groups of Americans.[35]

The 1932 Election

Part of the reason that Roosevelt was able to command such authority was that he was a skilled leader, orator, and communicator, with many years of political experience. The man, whom most Americans came to call simply FDR, was born into a wealthy New York family. From an early age, he lived a life of privilege and attended excellent private schools, including Harvard University. Roosevelt was also a fifth cousin of the twentieth-sixth president, Theodore Roosevelt (in office from 1901 to 1909), who became known as a great political reformer.

From his illustrious cousin, as well as from some of his teachers, the younger Roosevelt gained a strong desire to use his personal gifts and privileged position to serve the public. He served as a New York State senator from 1911 to 1913, for instance, and he followed with a stint as assistant secretary of the Navy during World War I. Not long after the war, Roosevelt tragically contracted polio and lost the use of his legs. Yet, in an impressive display of courage and determination, he reentered politics, serving as governor of New York during Hoover's presidential term.

Many Americans thought that Roosevelt was the most attractive candidate to represent the Democratic Party in the 1932 presidential election, and he won the party's nomination. Running against Hoover, he consistently used the deplorable conditions of the deepening Depression as fuel against the Republicans. The government needed to do more to alleviate the crisis, Roosevelt said, and to repair the broken economy. He reached out to the poor and jobless, members of organized labor, ethnic minorities, city dwellers, and others, trying to forge a widespread and diverse coalition that would support and elect him.

This strategy worked. In November 1932, Roosevelt won by a landslide, getting 472 electoral votes to Hoover's 59. (The popular vote was 22.8 million to 15.7 million.) The Democrats also cap-

A Peaceful Revolution

Roosevelt and his advisers believed that the New Deal represented an inevitable social and economic revolution in the United States. This revolution, as stated in 1935 by one of the chief administrators of the New Deal, Rex Tugwell, had the benefit of being peaceful and orderly.

A new deal [for the American people] was absolutely inevitable. People will submit to grave privations and will even starve peaceably, if they realize that actual dearth exists, but no man. . . will starve in the presence of abundance. The possibility of revolution, either peaceful or violent, against any system which denies the visible means of life to those who have produced those means, will always be with us. Therefore, the only choice before the American people. . . was whether their revolution should follow the course of violence and destruction or should express itself in orderly, legal channels. The answer was given in November 1932, when the American people gave to President Roosevelt a peaceful mandate to attempt to devise a better means of distributing the national income than had previously existed.

Rex Tugwell, "America Takes Hold of its Destiny," quoted in William Dudley, ed., *The Great Depression: Opposing Viewpoints*. San Diego: Greenhaven Press, 1994, pp.113–14.

tured both houses of Congress, winning the House by 310 to 117 and the Senate by 60 to 35. Clearly, Roosevelt had gained a mandate, authority granted by a large majority of citizens, to attack the Depression using any necessary means.

Trying to Dispel Fear

Roosevelt hinted at the nature and scope of this attack in his inaugural address, delivered on March 4, 1933. He refrained from the traditional political and feel-good rhetoric of such speeches. "I am certain," he said in a sober voice," that my fellow-Americans expect . . . [that] I will address them with a candor . . . which the present situation of our nation

impels. This is pre-eminently the time to speak the truth, the whole truth, frankly and boldly."

Before Americans could enact political and physical change, the new president asserted, they must adopt a major attitude change. They must face and conquer the nervous, gnawing state of fear that presently gripped the country. "The only thing we have to fear is fear itself," he declared in stirring tones, "nameless, unreasoning, unjustified terror which paralyzes needed efforts to convert retreat into advance." That advance could happen only by "treating the task as we would treat the emergency of a war," he said, and by making hard but essential sacrifices.

If we are to go forward, we must move as a trained and loyal army willing to sacrifice for the good of a common discipline, because, without such discipline, no progress is made, no leadership becomes effective. . . . I am prepared under my constitutional duty to recommend the measures that a stricken nation in the midst of a stricken world may require [and to] wage a war against the emergency as great as the power that would be given to me if we were in fact invaded by a foreign foe.[36]

Reactions to Roosevelt's speech were uniformly favorable. And after years of what many viewed as governmental inaction, a mood of optimism began to take hold across the land. The popular American humorist and political com-

In his 1933 inauguration speech, Franklin D. Roosevelt hinted at how he would deal with the Depression.

mentator Will Rogers captured that mood when he stated:

America hasn't been as happy in three years as they are today. No money, no banks, no work, no nothing, but they know they got a man in there who is wise to Congress, wise to our so-called big men. The whole country is with him, just so as he does something. Even if what he does is wrong, they are with him. Just so as he does something. If he burned down the Capitol, we would cheer and say, "Well, we at least got a fire started somehow."[37]

Indeed, Roosevelt and his advisers knew that they had to do what Rogers called "something." But what exactly should they do? The truth was that the country's economic crisis was so huge and dire that no one, not even the finest economists of the time, knew the best way to alleviate it. As a result, the new administration launched a bold, broad-based attack on the Depression. They initiated an enormous array of programs, most of them experimental to one degree or another, hoping that at least some would work. Thus, in contrast to Hoover's conservative, timid approach, in which government played a minimal role, Roosevelt assigned the federal government the chief role in the recovery.

The Bank Holiday

The first major move Roosevelt's government made was an attempt to stabilize

the value of U.S. currency, which had been declining, and restore confidence in the country's banks. On March 6, 1933, a mere two days after he had taken office, the president convened a special session of Congress. Standing before the legislators, he called for a national "bank holiday." All of the nation's banks would close down and allow U.S. Treasury accountants to inspect their books. This would reveal which banks were most in need of emergency aid. The government would grant such aid and then only those banks whose finances were sound enough would be allowed to reopen.

Though this was a daring and unprecedented move, most congressmen and senators felt it was necessary. So they passed it, many of them without even taking time to read the whole bill. The House of Representatives swiftly approved it by a voice vote, and a few hours later the Senate passed it nearly unanimously. Only seven hours after submitting the bill, Roosevelt signed it into law, marking the fastest passage of a piece of federal legislation in U.S. history.

Roosevelt realized that national legislators were not the only people whose support he needed to make the bank holiday a success. It was important for ordinary citizens, whose financial deposits banks sorely needed, to understand what was happening. So the president explained his strategy, on March 12, in the first of his "fireside chats." These were radio addresses in which he outlined national problems and challenges, and explained or defended government

President Franklin D. Roosevelt preparing for his first "fireside chat," in which he called for a national "bank holiday."

policies. "A question you will ask is this," he stated in the chat:

Why are all the banks not to be re-opened at the same time? The answer is simple. Your government does not intend that the history of the past few years shall be repeated. We do not want and will not have another epidemic of bank failures. As a result, we start tomorrow, Monday, with the opening of the banks ... which on first examination by the Treasury have already been found to be all right. . . . [In the days that follow, banks] all through the country will resume business. . . . Let me make it clear to you that if your bank does not open the first day, you are by no means justified in believing that it will not open.[38]

These reassuring words helped millions of Americans understand and ben-

The President Explains the Bank Holiday

In his first fireside chat, broadcast on March 12, 1933, President Roosevelt tried to reassure the American people by explaining the reasons for the bank holiday he had just declared.

First of all, let me state the simple fact that when you deposit money in a bank, the bank does not put the money into a safe deposit vault. It invests your money in many different . . . kinds of loans. In other words, the bank puts your money to work to keep the wheels of industry and agriculture turning around. . . . Because of undermined confidence on the part of the public, there was a general rush by a large portion of our population to turn bank deposits into currency or gold—a rush so great that the soundest banks could not get enough currency to meet the demand. . . . [So] I issued the proclamation providing for the nationwide bank holiday [which] is affording us the opportunity to supply the currency necessary to meet the situation. [There is no need to worry because] no sound bank is a dollar worse off than it was when it closed its doors on Monday.

Quoted in Franklin D. Roosevelt, *The Public Papers and Addresses of Franklin D. Roosevelt, Volume Two.* New York: Random House, 1938, pp. 61–62.

efit from the sweeping bank closures and reopenings. The new administration rapidly ended the national banking crisis, and restored public confidence in the country's banks. About a week after declaring the bank holiday, Roosevelt told an old friend, "We seem to be off to a good start and I hope to get through some important legislation while the feeling of the country is so friendly."[39]

The New Deal Begins

The president's use of the word "some" to describe the amount of legislation he was planning was an immense understatement. The number and magnitude of the federal programs he introduced in his first hundred days in office easily exceeded what some presidents had accomplished in their entire four-year terms. In the same month (March 1933) that he launched the bank holiday, Roosevelt called for the creation of two major new programs. One, the Agricultural Adjustment Administration (AAA), was both bold and controversial. Its purpose was to increase the profits of poor farmers by having them decrease the amount of grain, corn, rice, livestock, and other items they produced. The hope was that, as these commodities became more scarce, they would be worth more, and so their prices would increase, thereby allowing farmers to make more money.

Initial reactions to the AAA were mixed. Economists saw the wisdom of the plan. But many ordinary Americans objected to the idea of producing less food at a time when many people were starving. They especially disliked it when AAA officials ordered millions of farm animals slaughtered and thousands of acres of cotton plowed under to help raise prices and profits. As McElvaine puts it:

What sense did it make to destroy food in a nation where millions were hungry? . . . Very little, perhaps, but no less than it did to have poverty and want in the midst of abundance. . . . in the first place. The AAA concept of limiting production was no more incongruous [unfitting] than the economic system itself, which found no way to bring together idle workers and

An Agricultural Adjustment Administration (AAA) agent gunning down cattle. Many Americans disliked the idea of slaughtering millions of farm animals in order to raise prices and profits.

idle factories or hungry people and unsold crops.[40]

The other major New Deal program proposed in March 1933 was the Civilian Conservation Corps (CCC). Its goal was to provide work for the nation's many jobless young men between the ages of eighteen and twenty-five. In the eight years following its creation, the CCC paid some 2.7 million Americans to build dams, plant trees, fight forest fires, and so on, giving them both skills and the means to support their families. At the same time, the program helped to reduce the unemployment rate.

The Hundred Days also witnessed the birth of the Federal Emergency Relief

Roosevelt's Right-hand Man

One of the major architects of the New Deal, Harry Hopkins, was born in Iowa in 1890. As a young man, he served in various charitable and relief organizations, including the American Red Cross, and became a vocal advocate of child welfare. Franklin Roosevelt hired Hopkins to run New York state's relief organization in the Depression's early years. Then, in March 1933, Roosevelt, now president, made Hopkins director of the Federal Emergency Relief Administration (FERA). Later, Hopkins ran the Civil Works Administration (CWA) and Works Progress Administration (WPA). In keeping with his personal philosophy of aiding those in need, fully 90 percent of those Hopkins hired to run these agencies had previously been unemployed or on relief. Later, during World War II, and by now Roosevelt's right-hand man, Hopkins became the president's unofficial link to British prime minister, Winston Churchill, and helped ensure U.S.

Harry Hopkins was President Roosevelt's right-hand man and one of the major architects of the New Deal.

supplies of war materials to Britain. So close to the president that he actually lived in the White House for extended periods, Hopkins died of stomach cancer in January 1946.

Administration (FERA), created in May 1933. Roosevelt appointed his friend and chief advisor, Harry Hopkins, as director of this important new agency, designed to reduce adult unemployment. FERA gave funds to individual states for them to establish and run local work projects. In the span of only two and a half years, the program put more than 20 million people to work erecting buildings on public lands.

Still another of Roosevelt's daring and far-reaching programs was the Tennessee Valley Authority (TVA), created in May 1933. One of the largest construction projects in world history, it aimed to erect fifteen huge dams in the Tennessee River Valley. The structures, Roosevelt said, would give millions of Americans cheap electricity, help control damaging floods that occurred almost every year in the area, and provide years of work for tens of thousands of people. "This is the story of a great change," one of the TVA's directors, David E. Lilienthal, later said, describing the project with a somewhat poetic flair.

It is a tale of a wandering and inconstant river [which became a] chain of broad and lovely lakes, which people enjoy, and on which they can depend in all seasons. . . . It is the story of how waters once wasted and destructive have been controlled and now work, night and day, creating electric energy to lighten the burden of human drudgery. Here is a tale of fields . . . [grown] vigorous with new fertil-

ity . . . of forests now protected and refreshed . . . of people and how they have worked to create a new valley.[41]

The TVA was an overwhelming success. It supplied cheap electricity to some 8.5 million Americans, and provided long-term jobs for more than 200,000 people in the region.

While the World Watched

Ambitious as they were, the AAA, CCC, FERA, and TVA were not the only important programs the Roosevelt administration introduced in the historic Hundred Days. Some (though by no means all) of the others included the Economy Act (March 1933), intended to reduce the size of the federal government; the Truth-in-Securities Act (May), to reform the stock market and make future crashes less likely; and the Home Owner's Loan Act (June), to help people of limited means obtain mortgages.

This veritable blizzard of economic recovery activity raised the spirits of many Americans. The general view was that, even if some of these programs did not work, at least the government was making a valiant effort to turn things around. One of Roosevelt's advisors, Raymond Moley, later recalled:

During the whole "33 One-Hundred Days" Congress, people didn't [exactly] know what was going on. The public, couldn't understand these things that were being passed so fast. [But] they

Construction work being done on the site of a dam being built by the Tennessee Valley Authority (TVA), one of Roosevelt's New Deal initiatives.

knew something was happening, something good for them. They began investing and working and hoping again.[42]

Moreover, Americans were not the only ones closely watching Roosevelt's assault on the Depression. Most other countries were mired in the same financial slump. They hoped that America's ongoing economic experiments would be successful; for if they were, their effects would surely ripple outward and help everyone. The noted British politician, Winston Churchill, summed it up well. "The courage, the power, and the scale of his [Roosevelt's] effort," he said, "must enlist the ardent sympathy of every country. And his success could not fail to lift the whole world forward [into] the sunlight of an easier and more genial [happy] age."[43]

Chapter Four

A Grand Experiment: The New Deal

M any people in the United States and around the world were amazed at how many large-scale economic and social programs Roosevelt pushed through Congress in the Hundred Days (early March–early June 1933). Yet they soon learned that this flurry of legislative activity was only the beginning of the New Deal. In the years that followed, Roosevelt was reelected again and again. And he continued his big-government attack on the economic ravages of the Great Depression.

Backing Roosevelt up and supplying him with many of his ideas were the members of his so-called "Brain Trust." This was the term (coined sarcastically by *New York Times* writer, James M. Kiernan, in 1932) widely used to describe the president's closest advisers. Economists, college professors, and other highly educated individuals, they included Rex Tugwell, Raymond Moley,

Frances Perkins was a member of Roosevelt's "Brain Trust." Perkins became the first women to serve in a presidential cabinet when Roosevelt appointed her as secretary of labor.

Hugh S. Johnson, and Frances Perkins, among others. (Roosevelt appointed Perkins to the post of secretary of labor, making her the first woman ever to serve in a U.S. presidential cabinet.) These advisers were sometimes accused of being disorganized, idealistic, and wrongheaded. This was because the Brain Trusters, like the president they served, were not always sure exactly what they should do to combat the Depression. So they tried implementing many new, unprecedented, and sometimes risky, ideas in the hope that some would achieve success.

Indeed, the early Roosevelt era was unarguably a time of experimentation, of trying new ideas that seemed promising, even when one expected that some of these ideas would not work. Gardiner C. Means, who held high positions in several New Deal agencies, later remembered:

It was [a] yeastiness of experimentation that made the New Deal what it was. A hundred years from now, when historians look back on it, they will say a big corner was turned. People agreed that old things didn't work. What ran through the whole New Deal was finding a way to make things work. . . . We had meetings that would run into the early morning. A dozen of us sitting around a table,

Roosevelt's Charm

One reason that the majority of Americans supported the New Deal for so long was the confidence they had in President Roosevelt. In general, he was seen as a larger-than-life character who, though imperfect, was working hard for the nation's greater good. His secretary of labor, Frances Perkins, summed up this attitude in a book she wrote many years after the Depression's end.

People by instinct soon came to some conclusion about what he [Roosevelt] meant by a New Deal. Roosevelt liked people, [and] he had a way with them. They could see he liked them and people began to warm up to him. They didn't know him very well but they began to feel a kind of warmth toward him, due, as the newspapers say today, to his charm. Gradually there came to be a sense that the New Deal would be something warm and comfortable. You would be getting dealt out of whatever terrible predicament you were in—and the whole country was in a terrible predicament.

Frances Perkins, *Two Views of American Labor*. Los Angeles: Institute of Industrial Relations, 1965, p. 6.

thrashing out problems. . . . Everybody had a suggestion [and] there was no question in our minds that we were saving the country.[44]

This approach of remaking the nation through trial and error was a big part of the spirit of the New Deal and of the times. "Everybody was searching for ideas," New Deal economist, Joe Marcus, later wrote.

There was a search, a sense of values [that] would make a difference in the lives of people. . . . There were weaknesses [in the New Deal], but the point is, if you wanted to get jobs for people in a hurry . . . you had to find new [government leaders] with the spirit, with the drive.[45]

FDR's grand experiment in fighting the Depression, and reordering the economy and society, naturally produced both hits and misses. Some of his programs were very successful, others only marginally so, and still others complete failures. Regarding the New Deal's less successful ventures, one critic noted:

Many of [Roosevelt's] programs were turned on and off, started and stopped [as if he and his advisers were] shifting gears. . . . I was enthusiastic when Roosevelt came in, [but then] I became terribly disenchanted. He was a dramatic leader [with] charm [and] personality,

[but] to me he lacked the stick-to-it-iveness to carry a program through.[46]

Helping Those Most in Need

This observation proved to be partly right and partly wrong. It is true that a number of Roosevelt's New Deal programs did close down after only a few years in operation. However, some lasted for a decade or more, and a few were enormous successes that are still in operation today. One famous example is the Tennessee Valley Authority. Another is Social Security, now viewed as a cornerstone of American society.

The goal of the Social Security Act, implemented in August 1935, was, and still is, to help citizens who are in particular need because of increasing age, job loss, or sickness. Both employers and working people contribute to a special fund. The Social Security Administration then distributes the money to people who are older than sixty-five, temporarily unemployed, or too sick to work. When signing the act into law, Roosevelt said:

We can never insure one hundred percent of the population against one hundred percent of [life's] hazards, but we have tried to frame a law which will give some measure of protection to the average citizen and to his family against the loss of a job and against poverty-ridden old age.[47]

A 1936 poster providing information on how to apply for Social Security, a government program developed by President Roosevelt to help the elderly, unemployed, and disabled.

Although Social Security is universally accepted today, it was very controversial when Roosevelt and his advisers proposed it. Many people, especially conservatives, thought it entailed the government giving people money they had not directly earned. They worried that this was potentially harmful because it might promote various "un-American" values. Conservative Republican senator, Daniel O. Hastings of Delaware, for example, asserted that Social Security would make Americans lazy, spendthrift, and cowardly. "I fear it may end the progress of a great country," he said, and "discourage and defeat the American trait of thrift. It will go a long way toward destroying American initiative and courage."[48] James L. Donnelly, spokesman for the Illinois Manufacturers' Association, agreed. He warned that Social Security would undermine American life and values "by destroying initiative, discouraging thrift, and stifling individual responsibility."[49]

Roosevelt, and the many Americans who supported the idea of Social Security, argued that the new system did not simply give people free money. Every person who ever did any sort of work would pay a little into the system, they pointed out. Therefore, they would contribute to their own retirement. Also, the program was both humane and a wise way to help guard against future depressions and mass poverty. As Frances Perkins put it:

Our social security program will be a vital force working against the recurrence of severe depressions in the future. We can, as the principle of sustained purchasing power in hard times makes itself felt in every shop, store, and mill, grow old without being haunted by the specter of a poverty-ridden old age or of being a burden on our children. . . .

The American people want such security as the law provides. It will make this great republic a better and a happier place in which to live—for us, our children, and our children's children.[50]

Time has proven these words to be correct and shown that at least some of FDR's New Deal programs became positive forces for change.

Unemployment, 1933-1945

Year	Unemployed, in millions
1933	13
1934	11.4
1935	10.6
1936	9
1937	7.8
1938	10.3
1939	9.5
1940	8
1941	5.5
1942	2.6
1943	1
1944	.8
1945	1

Source: Cengage Learning, Gale.

Men working as part of the Civilian Conservation Corps (CCC), a government program designed to find decent-paying jobs for millions of young men.

Massive Job Creation

Some other New Deal initiatives that brought about positive change had the primary goal of putting millions of jobless Americans back to work. In this regard, the Civilian Conservation Corps (CCC), one of the first programs passed during the Hundred Days, was a huge success. A Gallup poll taken in April 1936 found that 82 percent of Americans strongly approved of the CCC because it found decent-paying work for millions of young men. The program lasted some nine years. And though it closed down in 1942, it would almost certainly have remained active, had it not been for the U.S. entrance into World War II; thereafter, most of the young men who would have found jobs through the CCC joined the military instead.

Millions of other Americans managed to find needed employment thanks to Roosevelt's Public Works Administration (PWA). This popular program was headed by a cabinet member, the secretary of the interior, Harold L. Ickes.

Known for his honesty, wit, organizational skills, and work ethic, Ickes was one of leading figures of the New Deal and of the U.S. government from 1933 to 1946. Under his guidance, the PWA struck deals with private contractors. They erected buildings and other public works with the goal of employing as many citizens as possible.

The sheer scope of the PWA's accomplishments was huge. Between 1933 and 1939, it employed half a million workers per year, who built the impressive total of some 34,500 streets, highways, schools, dams, airports, hospitals, sewage systems, tunnels, and Navy warships. Of

Harold L. Ickes

Harold Ickes (pronounced IK-is) was one of the leading U.S. government officials in the 1930s and 1940s, and a major administrator of the New Deal during the Depression era. Born in Pennsylvania in 1874, he first worked as a newspaper reporter. Soon he became a Republican political operative, who supported the policies of FDR's cousin, President Theodore Roosevelt. In 1933, Franklin Roosevelt, who wanted a Republican in his cabinet for the sake of balance, asked Ickes to serve as secretary of the interior. Ickes also ended up as director of the Public Works Administration (PWA), where he spent billions of dollars supplying unemployed Americans with jobs. Ickes was an ardent champion of civil liberties and civil rights, and for a time headed the Chicago branch of the National Association for the Advancement of Colored People (NAACP). He also courageously criticized the government's

Harold Ickes was a major administrator of President Roosevelt's New Deal programs during the Great Depression.

internment of Japanese Americans during World War II. Ickes resigned from the government early in 1946 and died in Washington, D.C., in 1952.

The Federal Writer's Project

Part of the Works Progress Administration, the Federal Writer's Project (FWP) was created on July 27, 1935. Its first director was the successful theatrical producer, Henry Alsberg. Over the course of several years, the FWP employed more than 6,600 writers, editors, historians, art critics, archaeologists, and others, who on average received $80 per week each. Their job was to compile or create local histories, oral histories, children's books, and other written documents that recorded or promoted American life and values. The agency's best-known products were forty-eight state guides published as part of the *American Guide Series*. Each book in the series provided a history of the state and descriptions of each of its cities and towns. Among the better-known writers who worked in the FWP were John Steinbeck, who later wrote *The Grapes of Wrath*; Studs Terkel, who later became famous for his oral history of the Depression era; black novelist Richard Wright; and noted female poet and playwright Mary Swenson.

these projects, about a third—11,428—were roads of various types; and 7,488 were schools. Among the best known public works the agency created are New York City's Lincoln Tunnel, Washington State's Grand Coulee Dam, and the Overseas Highway connecting Key West, Florida, to the U.S. mainland.

Even bigger in scope than the PWA was another New Deal program designed to put people to work—the Works Progress Administration (WPA). Created in May 1935, the WPA was, like the FERA, headed by Harry Hopkins. The WPA was the single largest New Deal program. At one time or another it employed about 8.5 million Americans in a wide range of professions. Like the PWA, the WPA built roads, bridges,

and airport runways. But the larger WPA also erected libraries, city halls, and parks, and devoted 7 percent of its budget to funding arts-related projects. Among the sub-programs of the WPA were the Federal Writer's Project, the Federal Theater Project, and the Federal Music Project. These and other similar programs sponsored some 250,000 concerts that played to audiences totaling 150 million people, and backed the creation of more than 475,000 pieces of original American art.

Regulating Industry

Most of these large-scale employment programs implemented during the New Deal were designed to create *new* jobs that would allow formerly unemployed

A sticker for the National Recovery Administration (NRA), which was designed to help both employees and employers.

people to earn money, some of which they would spend and thereby stimulate the depressed economy. Meanwhile, millions of other Americans already had jobs in existing industries and businesses. But many others who had specific skills in these industries had recently been laid off. Large numbers of big employers had cut back, partly because their businesses were disorganized, or not working to capacity, or exploiting their workers, or all of these things.

In an effort to make American industry more efficient and fair, and thereby get it to expand and hire more people, the Roosevelt administration proposed the National Industrial Recovery Act (NIRA). Congress passed it in June 1933. And its centerpiece became the National Recovery Administration (NRA), headed by a former military general, Hugh S. Johnson, who was also one of FDR's Brain Trusts. The NRA was de-

signed to help factories and other large businesses plan ahead better; to restore competition in the marketplace, which had diminished in the ailing economy; to regulate prices, so that industries could not overcharge consumers; to set the number of hours employees could work each week (to help reduce exploitation of the workers); and to eliminate child labor. McElvaine describes the NRA's major goals and how Johnson and his assistants expected to accomplish them:

The idea behind the NRA, quite simply, was to introduce rational planning into what had been a chaotic economic system. By providing balance to the economy, the NRA, it was hoped, would restore employment and prosperity. . . . Under the NRA, each industry in the country would draw up a code of practices that would be acceptable. These would cover wages, working conditions, . . . prices, and production. . . . In his second fireside chat [in May 1933], Roosevelt called the NRA "a partnership in planning" between business and government.[51]

These goals set by the NRA were big, diverse, and affected tens of millions of employers and employees at all levels of society. Collecting reliable statistics on changing situations in hundreds of thousands of businesses across the land was nearly impossible. So it is unclear how successful each aspect of the program was and how much it actually helped the economy. The consensus of historians is that, even though the NRA did not lift the country out the Depression in the 1930s, it was integral to the country's economic stability in the long

Civil Works Administration (CWA) workmen cleaning and painting the dome of the Denver Capitol. The CWA was the most notable failures of the New Deal programs.

run. "The NRA was one of most successful things the New Deal did," Gardiner Means pointed out.

> When it was created, American business was completely demoralized. Violent price-cutting and wage-cutting [was rampant and] nobody could make any plans for tomorrow. . . . The NRA changed the attitudes of business and the public. It revived the belief that something [positive] could be done.[52]

Frances Perkins added that the NRA created "a good relationship between government and labor. This was the first time that the government had realized its right, and even its duty, to consult with labor in regards to wages, hours, and other working conditions."[53]

Failures and Mistakes

Even if the NRA was only marginally successful, it achieved far more than some other New Deal ventures. The truth was that the grand economic and social experiment the New Deal embodied was bound to produce at least a few failures. Perhaps the most notable and debated example was the Civil Works Administration (CWA). Initiated in October 1933, the CWA was supposed to put millions of people to work immediately. As the historian, Don Nardo, has pointed out:

> At first, it seemed to be on the right track. By January 1934, the CWA

had more than 4.2 million people on its employment rolls. But the problem with the program was that it was too unstructured. A lot of people were receiving federal money for questionable or trivial endeavors—raking leaves, for example. And Roosevelt himself saw that the potential existed for creating a class of 'reliefers' who might become perpetually dependent on the government.[54]

In contrast, on the whole the CCC, and later the PWA and WPA, created more substantial and respectable jobs. As a result, in a rare move for a U.S. president, Roosevelt admitted he was wrong, and discontinued the CWA in April 1934.

Another, and much larger, mistake FDR committed during his implementation of the New Deal was his attempt to change the Supreme Court. Toward the close of his first term, the high court began striking down some of his progressive programs. Among those found to be unconstitutional were the NRA (in 1935) and AAA (in 1936). The president and most of his advisers held that these decisions were the result of too many old, conservative judges on the court, men born back in the mid-nineteenth century, who were old-fashioned and too suspicious of new and liberal ideas. In his ninth fireside chat, broadcast on March 9, 1937, Roosevelt told the American people:

> In the last four years, the sound rule of giving statutes the benefit of

THE INGENIOUS QUARTERBACK!

A political cartoon criticizing Roosevelt's Judiciary Reorganization Bill. Both Democrats and Republicans opposed the bill citing that it would give Roosevelt too much power.

all reasonable doubt has been cast aside. The [Supreme] Court has been acting not as a judicial body, but as a policy-making body. . . . The Court in addition to the proper use of its judicial functions has improperly set itself up as a third house of the Congress—a super-legislature, as one of the justices has called it—reading into the Constitution words and implications which are not there, and which were never intended to be there. We have, therefore, reached the point as a nation where we must take action to save the Constitution from the Court and the Court from itself.[55]

The action the president spoke of took the form of the Judiciary Reorganization Bill of 1937. His political opponents were hardly wrong when they called it the "court-packing bill." It called for giving the president the right to appoint an extra judge for each sitting judge who was older than seventy and a half. Naturally, each of these extra judges would be hand-picked for his loyalty to FDR and his ideas. Considering the configuration of the Court at the time, this would have expanded it from nine to fifteen judges, and ensured that most or all of Roosevelt's programs would thereafter be deemed constitutional.

The bill raised an outcry from many Republicans and Democrats alike. Opponents worried that it would give the office of president too much authority, and create an imbalance of power among the three branches of govern-ment (executive, legislative, and judicial). Accordingly, the Senate rejected the idea. "This bill [is] a needless, futile, and utterly dangerous abandonment of constitutional principle," the senators said. "It is a proposal without precedent and without justification. It would subjugate the courts to the will of Congress and the President and thereby destroy the independence of the judiciary."[56]

FDR lost his bid to reshape the Supreme Court, therefore. However, for reasons that are still unclear and debated, the high court began to vote more often in his favor anyway. Thus, most elements of the New Deal remained in place and continued to battle the Depression, which had not yet relinquished its cruel hold on the country and the world.

Chapter Five

Life and Leisure During the Depression

If one could sum up in a few descriptive phrases the daily lives of average Americans during the Great Depression, two of those phrases would surely be "grinding poverty" and "trying to make ends meet." The sad fact was that the vast majority of people in the country were either poor or nearly so. This was partly because so many people were out of work—on average 25 percent of wage earners (15 to 20 million people) in 1933. Also, many of those lucky enough to retain their jobs suffered severe salary cuts. Wage reductions of 40 to 60 percent were not unusual. In the same period, some 9 million American families lost their life savings in bank failures.

With little or no money coming in, millions of American families did the best they could to make do and survive. Typical of many rural poor families was that of George Stockard of southern Texas. He was sixteen when the Depression hit and shared a small farmhouse with fifteen relatives. He later recalled:

We had no water whatever. We'd have to go to town and buy it for 5 cents a gallon. We took the wagon, not being able to afford the 7 cents a gallon for gasoline. Clothes were washed at a community [well], which was a dirty place with filthy water. It made the clothes smell something awful.[57]

Similarly sad was this snippet filed by a newspaper reporter after visiting rural North Dakota in 1932:

Last winter the temperature went down to 40 below zero and stayed there for ten days, while a 60-mile wind howled across the plains. And entering that kind of winter we have between 4,000 and 5,000 human beings . . . without clothing or bedding, getting just enough

A line of unemployed men wait outside a Depression-era soup kitchen in Chicago. Lines like this were a daily occurrence in most of America's large cities.

food to keep them from starving. No fuel. Living in houses that a prosperous farmer wouldn't put his cattle in.[58]

The situation in America's cities was little different. Thousands of urban dwellers were either temporarily or permanently homeless. Every day, tens of thousands of people stood in soup-

or breadlines, hoping to stave off hunger. Not surprisingly, such conditions caused a lot of worry, fear, and mental depression, and an estimated 20,000 distraught individuals committed suicide in 1931 alone.

Considering the depth of poverty and unhappiness in the country, one might expect there to be little interest in or spending on games, movies, and other leisure activities. Yet the reality was exactly the opposite. Precisely because they had so little to be happy about, Americans felt a desperate need to escape, even if only for an hour or two a week, from the bleakness of their lives. The results of these quite natural feelings were remarkable. The 1930s, perhaps the darkest and most miserable decade in the country's history, witnessed an outpouring of leisure pursuit that remains unmatched before or since.

Looking for a Job

One particularly bleak reality that many people wanted to escape from, but could not, was unemployment. Few jobs were available before Roosevelt's PWA, WPA, and other similar programs began putting people back to work. As successful as these programs were, they did not eradicate joblessness. In 1935, for example, the unemployment rate was still a crippling 20 percent; and as late as 1940, it remained high at 14.6 percent.

The ritual of job-hunting, therefore, became a prominent and familiar fea-

Suicides in the United States, 1930-1945

Year	Number
1930	18,323
1932	20,646
1935	18,214
1940	18,907

Source: Cengage Learning, Gale.

ture of Depression life in towns and cities across the land. In fact, large numbers of men, who far outnumbered women as breadwinners at the time, relentlessly searched for work, even when they knew no jobs existed. One reason for this seemingly obsessive-compulsive behavior was a sturdy but harsh work ethic that had long before become ingrained in American society. Essentially, it held that a man was not worthy—not a "real man"—if he lacked a job and could not support his family. "Americans had been brought up on the belief that meaningful work is the basis of life," McElvaine points out.

> A widespread attitude of the unemployed early in the Depression was "There must be something wrong with a fellow who can't get a job. Sure, I've lost my job, but I'm still a worthy provider. Work will turn up soon." Every morning, up before dawn, washed, shaved, and dressed as neatly as possible. To the factory gates, only to find a hundred others already there, staring blankly at the sign: NO HELP WANTED. To search then became more feverish.[59]

It did not help that the harsh conditions of their lives caused job-hunters to look older and more haggard, making it even harder for them to find work. An Oklahoma woman explained the problem in a 1934 letter to FDR's wife, Eleanor Roosevelt:

The unemployed have been so long without food, clothes, shoes, medical care, dental care, etc., [that] we look pretty bad. So when we ask for a job we don't get it. And we look and feel a little worse each day. When we ask for food, they call us bums.[60]

"Bums" was only one of many derogatory terms commonly used against unemployed men and women during the Depression. Sadly, people without jobs were sometimes the victims of prejudice by people fortunate enough to have steady work. Typical epithets aimed at poverty-stricken men and their families were: "good-for-nothing loafers," "thieves," "lazy, immoral people," "human parasites," and "pampered poverty-rats."[61]

Even more pitiful was that some of the jobless men who endured these abuses came to believe that they must indeed be

Men line up in front of New York City Hall to apply for jobs cleaning snow from city streets. Across the United States, job-hunting became a familiar ritual in Depression-era towns and cities.

worthless. And for some the only way out appeared to be suicide. Joseph L. Heffernan, mayor of Youngstown, Ohio, during the Depression's early years, remembered an unemployed man who came to him asking for work:

One man I had known for years stood at my desk and calmly said, "My wife is frantic. After working at the steel mill for twenty-five years, I have lost my job, and I'm too old to get other work. If you can't do something for me, I'm going to kill myself."[62]

This man fortunately found a job and did not end up taking his own life. But a mechanic living in Houston, Texas was not so lucky. Before killing himself, he left this note:

This depression has got me licked. There is no work to be had. I can't accept charity and I am too proud to appeal to my kin or friends, and I am too honest to steal. So I see no other course. A land flowing with milk and honey and a first class mechanic can't make an honest living. I would rather take my chances with a just God than with unjust humanity.[63]

Regarding those who resorted to such desperate measures, some simple figures tell an awful tale. The U.S. national suicide rate rose from 14 per 100,000 in 1929 to 17.4 per 100,000 in 1932. Moreover, the rate was much higher in many cities; in

Minneapolis, for instance, it peaked at 26.1 per 100,000 in 1932.

Changing Family Roles

Large-scale unemployment and poverty also upset traditional family roles in communities across the country. The usual status and responsibilities of men, women, and children in these families changed, sometimes markedly so. In particular, the status of the man as the chief breadwinner and head of the family diminished. Before the Depression, a man could claim dominance because he supported the family. But when he could no longer do so, society, and often he himself, saw it as a sort of demotion in rank.

In addition, many men found themselves hanging around the house, and, in a sense, intruding into what had long been the women's sphere. One positive result of this trend was that many men learned to see things more from a woman's perspective, as McElvaine points out:

In certain respects, the Depression can be seen as having effected a "feminization" of American society. The self-centered, aggressive, competitive "male" ethic of the 1920s was discredited. Men who lost their jobs became dependent in ways that women had been thought to be. . . . [Many men] also moved toward [more] "feminine" values . . . [such as] Depression victims tended to [try to better themselves] through "female" values. They sought to

Traditional family roles changed during the Depression as men were forced to stay at home due to large-scale unemployment across the country.

escape dependence not through "male," self-centered, "rugged" individualism, but through cooperation and compassion.[64]

In some families, however, the intrusion of unemployed men into the traditional female sphere had negative consequences. Some couples, thrown together day and night and suffering from various kinds of stress, quarreled more often. In some cases, a husband was unable to find work, but his wife or oldest son did manage to get a job. This hurt the man's pride and he became depressed, despondent, and/or more likely to lash out violently at relatives.

Children suffered, too. Parents under stress frequently passed their own worries on to their sons and daughters. During the early years of the Depression, a New York kindergarten teacher remarked:

> The children all seem to be so excitable and high-strung these days. I cannot help thinking it's due to the distress at home.[65]

At least these children were in school. Many others were not because financial woes forced numerous towns and cities across the nation to close some of their schools. Other children had to quit school to help their parents make ends meet. Boys worked in fields or helped repair aging and ailing family vehicles. Girls helped their mothers make or mend clothes and looked after younger siblings. In all, some 3 million children between the ages of seven and seventeen left school in the 1930s. Some of them managed to find work outside the home through FDR's Civilian Conservation Corps, but many who quit school remained jobless for years, and an estimated 200,000 of them became panhandlers (beggars).

Escape into Make-believe

Whether one had a job or not during the Depression, making ends meet and surviving from one week to the next was life's major priority. But no matter how hard things got, most people somehow managed to squeeze out enough time and money to have some fun when they could. In fact, Americans pursued a wide range of leisure and entertainment activities all through the 1930s. Sporting events, including baseball and football games, were widely popular. So were holiday parades and picnics, high school band concerts, community dances, county fairs, and carnivals that traveled from town to town.

However, by far the most popular form of escapist entertainment in that era was going to the movies. Nearly every town in the country had at least one small movie theater. These places were nearly always packed. Indeed, between 80 and 90 million Americans—more than 60 percent of the entire population of the United States—attended a movie at least once a week during the 1930s. (In comparison, 25 to 30 million Americans, making up about 10 percent of the population, attend movies each week today.) The main reason that so many people could afford it was that tickets were inexpensive—on average 10 to 20 cents for adults and 5 to 10 cents for children. Moreover, moviegoers got a lot more for their money. For the price of admission, most theaters ran two full-length movies, one or two cartoons, and a short newsreel summarizing national and world events of the past week.

Depression-era Americans were also drawn to movie theaters by the specific subject matter of films. For the most part, they did not enjoy screen stories that depicted everyday life in a realistic fashion because it reminded them too much of their personal troubles. Rather, most moviegoers preferred to be transported into a world of make-believe. Musicals, such as *Forty-Second Street* (1933) and *The Gold Diggers* (1935), were widely popular, therefore. So were Westerns, including those featuring singing cowboys like Gene Autry and Tex Ritter. The most popular Western of the decade was *Stagecoach* (1939), directed by John Ford and starring the then thirty-two-year-old John Wayne. Moviegoers also flocked to see gangster films like *Little Caesar* (1931); horror films like *Frankenstein* (1931); silly comedies like *Bringing up Baby* (1938); and "costume epics" such as *The Adventures of Robin Hood* (1938) and *Gone With the Wind* (1939).

Listening and Dancing One's Cares Away

Another advantage of going to the movies in the Depression era was that it was a social experience. Before and after the films were shown, people got to share the latest gossip with their neighbors or to meet new friends. A less social, but almost as popular, activity was listening to the radio. Nearly every home, even most poor ones, had a radio, just as almost every American home today has a television set.

Radio listeners of the 1930s tuned in for music and news, of course. But they also enjoyed weekly, and sometimes nightly, sitcoms, dramas, mysteries, detective shows, and other episodic programs similar to those later seen on TV. (In fact, a number of popular radio shows, such as comedian Jack Benny's zany sitcom, which premiered in 1932, became popular television programs in the 1950s.) Unarguably the most popular radio show of the decade was "Amos 'n Andy," a nightly comedy about a black big-city cab driver named Amos and his friend Andy, who regularly found themselves in various humorous social situations. More than 40 million people,

"Tomorrow is another day!"

Depression-era Americans went to see Gone With the Wind in droves in 1939, making this American Civil War epic the most successful movie of the decade, and one of the most popular films of all time. Part of the appeal to 1930s audiences was the onscreen dilemma of the main character, Scarlet O'Hara (played by Vivian Leigh). Originally a rich, spoiled southern belle, she lost everything in the Civil War, which forced her to start over from scratch, with only her wits and courage to guide her. This predicament closely mirrored the experiences of many Americans in the 1930s. And Scarlet's famous last, defiant, and optimistic line, "Tomorrow is another day!" was a fitting message of hope to end a decade during which so many Americans had concluded that all hope was lost.

Many Depression-era Americans related to the character Scarlet O'Hara from the film Gone With the Wind, *and as a result made the movie one of the most successful films of all time.*

The Brains Behind Bingo

Of the many games that people played in the 1930s to help forget their troubles, one of the most popular was Bingo, still widely played today. Several earlier versions of the game had been widely played in the early years of the twentieth century, among them Beano, Lucky, and Fortune. But the brains behind the version that swept America in the Depression was a New York toy salesman named Edwin Lowe. A big fan of Beano, he played it often with friends. On one occasion, one of them was so excited when she won that she spontaneously cried out, "B-B-Bingo!" Lowe realized this would be a good name to market, so he did so, insisting that anyone who held a public Bingo game pay him a dollar.

Lowe also hired a math expert to compile a larger array of number combinations for the Bingo cards, which made the game more difficult to win than Beano and earlier versions. In addition, Lowe paid a factory to make millions of printed game cards and wooden tokens. Thereafter, public Bingo games attracted big crowds throughout the 1930s. In the largest on record, held in 1934 in Teaneck, New Jersey, some 60,000 people played the game at the same time.

one third of all Americans, listened to the show each night at the height of the Depression.

One thing that movies and radio had in common was that they cost money. One had to buy a ticket to see a movie, and buy the household radio. In contrast, in an era in which money was scarce, it is perhaps not surprising that many people tried to combine money-making and leisure activities. Gambling, including card games, blackjack, and other casino-type games, were extremely popular, for example. People also liked to bet on the outcomes of pinball games, as pinball machines were first introduced in the United States in the early 1930s.

Another way that people tried to have fun and strike it rich at the same time was by participating in dance marathons. Also called dance "derbies," these were public competitions in which several couples began dancing at a given signal. The object was to see which couple could continue dancing the longest without falling asleep or collapsing onto the dance floor. (In some contests, one dancer was permitted to fall asleep as long as the other could hold him or her up and keep dancing.) Eventually, one couple after another quit from sheer exhaustion, until, after days or even weeks, one couple was left. The longest marathon dance recorded in the 1930s was an incredible 22 weeks, 3½ days. Prizes at the larger dance contests ran from several hundred up to several thousands

A couple dancing during a 1939 dance marathon. These marathons were a way for people to forget about their problems during the Depression.

dollars, a lot of money during the Depression.

The less glamorous aspect of dance marathons was that the participants risked their health or even their lives. With little or no sleep and lacking regular meals for days or weeks on end, many became sick and at least two actually died. As a result, by the late 1930s most states had outlawed these bizarre contests. Clearly, these public spectacles were a symptom of the hard times that then prevailed, when many people were willing to do almost anything to temporarily forget their troubles and/or make some extra money.

Chapter Six

Women and Minorities in the Depression

Although most Americans were negatively impacted by the Great Depression, certain sectors of society were worse off than others. Those who suffered the most, on the whole, were members of what have traditionally been viewed as either minority or disadvantaged groups. These included women, blacks, Native Americans, various immigrant and ethnic groups, and impoverished migrant workers. They had two major obstacles to their getting ahead in life—the economic bad times brought on by the Depression and ingrained prejudice. Some of President Roosevelt's New Deal programs made an attempt to address the problems these people faced. But good intentions and the stroke of a legislative pen could not erase centuries of deep-seated biases and stereotyping. So the New Deal was in most cases only mar-

ginally effective in alleviating the plight of minorities.

Depression-era Women

Nevertheless, some members of these groups did make some measurable gains during the 1930s. In the case of American women, these gains were primarily ceremonial, symbolic, and confined to a few women in highly visible public positions, mainly appointed by the president to various government posts. Besides Frances Perkins, the first female U.S. cabinet member, they included Ruth Bryan Owen, the first woman ambassador (to Denmark); Marion Glass Banister, the first U.S. Assistant Treasurer; and Florence Allen, the first female judge to sit on the U.S. Circuit Court of Appeals. Women also ran some of the New Deal programs. Hallie Flanagan directed the Federal Theater Project, for instance, and Mary McLeod Bethune headed the Office of Minority Affairs for the National Youth Administration. (Bethune was also the first black American to head a federal government agency.)

The most visible woman of all in the government in the Depression era, of course, was the First Lady. As historian Susan Ware explains, Eleanor Roosevelt did much to advance the status of American women:

Eleanor Roosevelt believed in women's capabilities, and she supported women's causes. She was

Mary McLeod Bethune: Distinguished American

One of the leading American black figures of the 1920s and 1930s, Mary McLeod Bethune was born in South Carolina in 1875. Her parents were former slaves who had been freed at the close of the Civil War. A brilliant and hard-working student, young Mary earned scholarships to attend excellent schools in North Carolina and Illinois. She soon earned a name as an educator of the first rank. In 1904, Bethune established a school in Daytona Beach, Florida, which eventually became Bethune-Cookman College. She served as president of the college from 1923 to 1942 and again from 1946 to 1947. Partly because of her friendship with the First Lady, Eleanor Roosevelt, President Roosevelt

President Roosevelt placed Mary McLeod Bethune in charge of the Division of Negro Affairs, making her the first black American to head a government agency.

placed Bethune in charge of the Division of Negro Affairs in a New Deal program, the National Youth Administration (NYA). This made Bethune the first black American to head a government agency. In 1945, Roosevelt's successor, Harry S Truman, appointed her as one of several distinguished consultants who helped to set up the fledgling United Nations (UN) in New York City. Bethune died of a heart attack in 1955. Her house was later preserved by the National Park Service as the Mary McLeod Bethune Council House National Historic Site, in Washington, D.C.

especially useful to other women administrators in Washington by providing White House access to women who had a program or idea that they wanted brought to the attention of the president. . . . [She] could also command public attention in her own right through press conferences and her newspaper column. . . . It is practically impossible to imagine so much progress for women in the New Deal without Eleanor Roosevelt in the White House.[66]

The progress for women outside the inner corridors of the New Deal was not nearly so marked, however. In fact, most American women made only minimal headway against general prejudices during the 1930s. This was partly because of longstanding social traditions that viewed men as the breadwinners and heads of households. But it was also because many people thought that working women were taking jobs away from men, and thereby hurting both families and the country. This attitude explains why 77 percent of the nation's school districts refused to hire married women. As late as 1939, moreover, 84 percent of insurance companies, 65 percent of banks, and 63 percent of public utility companies had rules against hiring women. Some men were particularly brazen about discouraging female employment. "Simply fire the women, who shouldn't be working anyway, and hire the men," noted journalist Norman Cousins de-

clared. "Presto! No unemployment. No relief rolls. No Depression."[67]

Such simple-minded statements masked the reality that it was not always so simple a matter as women filling jobs that rightfully belonged to men. Quite often women did work that men did not traditionally do and that many men actually refused to do, even if they had to remain out of work and stand in breadlines. One fifth of all female workers during the Depression era were maids and other domestic servants, for example. In the 1930s, live-in maids made the pitiful wage of $8 a week in New York City, the highest paying area in the country for domestic workers.

Furthermore, even when women did do jobs that men were willing to take, women made considerably less money for the same amount of work. The average annual pay of an employed woman in the 1930s was $525, compared with $1,027 for a man. Even many of FDR's New Deal programs, including those headed by women, discriminated against women by failing to grant them equal pay with men. Men working on most WPA projects made $5 a day, for instance, whereas women who worked on the same projects and did comparable work received $3 a day. True, wage-earning codes set by the National Recovery Administration helped women workers by guaranteeing them a minimum wage. But the female minimum wage was always lower than the male version.

Not all women held jobs during the Depression, of course. Many stayed

A women working as a cook during the Great Depression. During the 1930s, one-fifth of all female workers were employed as maids or other domestic workers.

home, where they cooked, cleaned, raised children, worked in fields, and did the best they could to make ends meet in the brutal economy. Though these women had done nothing to threaten the male job market, they were nevertheless victimized by ingrained gender biases. Women were at first treated unfairly by the Social Security Act, for example. Before 1939, the program helped only the wage earners themselves, who were most often men. If a male worker died, his stay-at-home wife could not collect *any* of his benefits and found herself shut out of the system. Even when the government amended the law in 1939, unemployed women were allowed to collect only half of their deceased husbands' benefits.

Thus, whether they worked or not, American women in the 1930s were still second-class citizens, who benefited only minimally from the New Deal's broad social programs, as Ware says:

> The treatment of women by relief agencies and New Deal policies parallels a pattern applicable to most aspects of the New Deal. Those women whom it helped never forgot the aid they received from the federal government, but many received little or nothing at all. This applied to both men and women, but women had to struggle even harder to get their due.[68]

The First Fired and Last Hired

The very real societal prejudices white women encountered during the Depres-

sion were relatively tame in comparison to those felt by black women, and by black men as well. Racism was still strong in America in those days, especially in the South. Blacks, then more commonly called Negroes, were widely considered inferior to whites, even to the poorest and most uneducated whites.

At the height of the Depression, therefore, when jobs were few and far between, many whites resented seeing blacks get any kind of work. These whites believed that whites should have the first pick of all jobs. Before the onset of the Depression, black men frequently did jobs that many white men would not take or did not want; these included domestic servant, elevator operator, garbage collector, waiter, street cleaner, and so on. When the economy collapsed, more whites were willing to take these jobs and demanded that blacks quit or be fired to make way for whites. Some white people in Atlanta began using the mean-spirited slogan: "No jobs for [blacks] until every white man has a job." And a white store clerk in Marianna, Florida said: "A [black person] hasn't got no right to have a job when there are white men who can do the work and are out of work."[69]

One result of such blatant racism was that Depression-era blacks were, more often than not, the first to get fired and the last to get hired.

In 1932, with the country's overall unemployment figure climbing toward 25 percent, the unemployment rate for blacks was already 50 percent. At the time, about half of America's 12 million

During the Depression, it was even more difficult for blacks, like these unemployed steel workers, to find employment.

blacks lived in rural areas and roughly 40 percent worked in agricultural jobs. (Less than 20 percent of black farmers then owned the land they worked on.) As the decade wore on, white land owners evicted many of their black tenant farmers in order to save money. So there were 192,000 fewer black tenant farmers in 1940 than in 1930. Moreover, even those blacks who had agricultural jobs made far less money than whites in the same jobs. In 1934, black farmers had an average income of $200 or less per year, three to five times lower than the average income of white farmers.

Summarizing the uphill battle that American blacks faced in the early 1930s, the journalist, Edwin P. Hoyt, said:

Negroes secured a special justice in America—harsher than the justice meted out to whites. They performed the same work alongside white workers, and received less pay for it. . . . Few Negroes took any interest in education or self-improvement because they had learned from painful experience that no matter how much they exercised their brains, there was a low ceiling of accomplishment for Negroes in the white community.[70]

Roosevelt's secretary of the interior, Harold Ickes, a staunch advocate of improving the lot of blacks, added:

The Negro has met with many abuses and obstacles. . . . For generations, he has been exploited by corrupt politicians, who have bought his vote or have made him promises which were never expected to be kept.[71]

A black Alabama cotton farmer named Nate Shaw was more blunt. "The colored

Fears Fueled by Racism

In his collection of oral tales about the Depression era, Studs Terkel recorded remarks by John Beecher, a poet who wrote about Depression life. In the interview, Beecher remembered some blatant incidents of prejudice against blacks during the implementation of the New Deal.

When the government came in and started to build a model camp for Negroes [in Florida], with screened shelters and shower baths and flush toilets, and an infirmary, a community center, a school, and playgrounds . . . [local whites] raised hell. What was the government's idea, anyway, ruining the rental value [of their own nearby quarters]? The Negroes wouldn't use the [new] camp, [the whites argued]. They liked to be dirty; they liked to be diseased; they liked to be vicious. When the [whites] saw that the government was going ahead anyway, they said: "You'll have to hire a bunch of camp guards, white guards, and have them control the camp with clubs and pistols, or the Negroes won't pay the rent. Or they'll stop working entirely and they'll take the camp to pieces." [None of these things happened. The Negro camp proved to be a success. No guards were posted and everyone paid their rent.]

Quoted in Studs Terkel, *Hard Times: An Oral History of the Great Depression*. New York: Random House, 2000, p. 280.

man [has] just been a dog for this country for years and years, " he said.[72]

Blacks in the New Deal

As bleak as it was for American blacks during the Depression, as a group they did make what turned out to be historically important strides during that era. In fact, under some of FDR's New Deal programs, in the span of only a few years, blacks made more economic and social gains than they had in the entire six decades following the Civil War. These gains were minimal, to be sure; when the Depression ended in the early 1940s, blacks were still second-class citizens suffering under an enormous load of prejudice. Yet it was because of Roosevelt and the New Deal that the idea of black equality began to be voiced in a serious manner in America. And modern historians trace the modest beginnings of the Civil Rights movement that blossomed in the 1950s and 1960s back to the 1930s.

It is somewhat unclear what FDR thought about blacks in his heart and in private thoughts and conversations. But in his public speeches and policies, he at least attempted to treat black Americans more fairly, more equally, and with more dignity than they had been accorded in the past. Roosevelt abolished segregation in federal offices in Washington, D.C., and began racially to integrate the armed forces. He also appointed black men and women as advisers on race relations in the main offices of several New Deal programs.

The president made these moves, then viewed as quite bold, partly because he had surrounded himself with progressive, fair-minded individuals like Ickes. But Roosevelt's attitudes about race relations and equality were influenced even more by his wife. Eleanor Roosevelt became a staunch advocate for the rights of American minorities, including blacks. To a large degree, her tolerant attitudes and knowledge about black problems came from her close friendship with Mary McLeod Bethune, who long served as FDR's chief adviser on minority issues. The first lady also learned much about the plight of blacks from another black friend, Walter White, the first black national secretary of the National Association for the Advancement of Colored People (NAACP), which had been established in 1909. Some evidence suggests that Eleanor Roosevelt proceeded to educate her husband, already a progressive thinker, about the need for reforming race relations. A major Pennsylvania newspaper later reported:

> Though her husband as president was given credit for sympathizing with the plight and aspirations of Negroes, it has since become apparent that it was she who made him conscious of the social prejudices existing in the country.[73]

As a result, some New Deal job programs, including the PWA and CCC, became to a small but significant degree instruments of social justice. These agen-

Although minimal, black Americans did make small strides toward equality, and some affluence, during Roosevelt's administration.

cies mandated paying black men the same wages as white men for the same work. Many whites complained about such equal treatment, and demanded that blacks be paid less than whites. At one point, the president responded by pointing out that black workers had to support their families just as white workers did; and how could blacks be expected to make "a reasonable American standard of living,"[74] if they made far less money than whites. Roosevelt also courageously responded to racist remarks and demands by employing some 200,000 black men through the CCC and appointing thirty-nine black reserve officers and 152 black educational advisers in that program.

Blacks also benefited mightily from loans obtained from the Farm Security Administration (FSA), a New Deal agency that lent money to needy farmers. Fully 23 percent of its loans went to blacks. "One could argue," historian Raymond Wolters writes, "that even this share was inadequate because the Negro's needs were so much greater" than those of whites. "It is nevertheless a tribute to the fair-mindedness of the FSA's administrators that Negroes received as large a share of farm security benefits as they did."[75]

It must not be construed by such successes, however, that the New Deal was a panacea, or cure, for long underprivileged black Americans. Racism was still alive and well in the United States. And no matter how well meaning Roosevelt and his chief administrators were, blatant discrimination existed in many New Deal programs. Abuses of blacks in hiring, firing, wages, housing, and other areas were reported in various PWA projects, and particularly in the TVA. New Deal administrators typically responded to criticisms of these abuses by saying that the fault lay with ingrained prejudices, not Roosevelt's government. For example, Ickes said, "the prejudices that have been fostered and built up for 60 years cannot be done away with overnight."[76]

Addressing the Plight of American Indians

Longstanding prejudices against Native Americans, in the 1930s more commonly called American Indians, were also impossible to erase quickly. But the New Dealers must be given credit for making an earnest effort to better the lives of Indians. When the Depression hit, most Indians had already been confined to reservations for several decades. And during those years, the federal government had been pursuing a policy of assimilation; this entailed slowly trying to absorb Indians into white society and thereby eradicate traditional Indian cultures. The policy was poorly applied, not very successful, and actually intensified prejudice against Indians. In 1928, less than a year before the great stock market crash, a government investigator reported: "An overwhelming majority of the Indians are poor, even extremely poor, and they are not adjusted to the [culture and] system of the dominant white civilization."[77] Moreover, the plight of American Indians only got

Blackfoot Indians dressed in traditional clothing during a 1930s tribal gathering. New Deal programs resulted in small improvements in the lives of American Indians.

worse as the Depression tightened its grip on the country's economy.

This deplorable situation fortunately began to change in 1933, when the Roosevelt administration launched the New Deal. John Collier, an idealistic California social worker, became the U.S. Commissioner of Indian Affairs. Collier rightly recognized that the assimilation policy was racist and destructive, and launched a new policy that aimed to preserve tra-

ditional Indian cultures. This goal was the central feature of the 1934 Indian Reorganization Act (IRA). It strengthened tribal governments, encouraged the expansion of Indian commercial endeavors to create self-reliance, and helped secure education loans for Indians.

Collier realized that, though the IRA would give Indians a major boost in the long run, in the short run they badly needed jobs. So he personally organized the Indian Emergency Conservation Work Program (IECW), funded as a branch of the CCC. Employed on or near reservations, thousands of Indians planted forests, battled soil erosion, and built roads and fire lookout stations. The program was so popular among Indians that at one point some five hundred Cherokees applied for a hundred job openings.

Ethnic Minorities and Poor Migrants

While Indians struggled to support their families and preserve their cultures in the midst of sometimes hostile whites, ethnic minorities from other lands also experienced prejudice. In the three decades preceding the onset of the Depression, millions of immigrants had come to the United States from Italy, Greece, Poland, Hungary, Germany, Russia, and numerous other countries. They received a mixed reception. Some Americans welcomed them and helped them assimilate, while others saw them as intruders out to steal jobs from "real Americans." The latter attitude intensified during the Depression, when jobs became much scarcer. A number of immigrants, or their American-born children, found themselves the targets of

An immigrant family eating Christmas dinner. During the Depression hostility toward European immigrants intensified as they became competitors for jobs.

ethnic biases and slurs. George Tallen, of Moberly, Missouri, whose parents had been born in Greece, later recalled:

In Moberly, I was called a god-d _ _ _ _ _ Greek. People would lean out of the car window and tell me to go back where I came from. The same for other national groups, mostly from eastern and southern Europe. . . . Jews—they had a bad time. My father told me to pay no attention. He said, "Do your work, do good at school, behave yourself, and laugh when people [try] to berate you."[78]

Even some non-immigrant whites became targets of prejudice during the Depression era, again partly based on fears that they would take others' jobs. The so-called Oakies were the most famous example. They were the principal victims of the Dust Bowl, a series of disastrous dust storms in the 1930s that ravaged the great plains, where poor agricultural techniques and severe drought had turned large tracts of fertile soil to dust. More than half a million residents of the region fled to other states. An estimated 15 percent of Oklahomans, along with people from other Dust Bowl states, moved to California. Although not all the migrants were from Oklahoma, all collectively became known as Oakies, which soon became a derogatory term. "They were promptly stereotyped, exactly like a racial minority," editor and

Steinbeck on the Oakies

Noted American novelist, John Steinbeck, captured the plight of the migrant workers, who came to be called Oakies, in this moving excerpt from his classic novel The Grapes of Wrath.

And then the dispossessed were drawn west—from Kansas, Oklahoma, Texas, New Mexico; from Nevada and Arkansas families, tribes, dusted out, tractored out. Carloads, caravans, homeless and hungry; twenty thousand and fifty thousand and a hundred thousand and two hundred thousand. They streamed over the mountains, hungry and restless. . . . The kids are hungry. We got no place to live. Like ants scurrying for work, for food, and most of all for land. . . . And the dispossessed, the migrants, flowed into California, two hundred and fifty thousand, and three hundred thousand. Behind them . . . [other] tenants were being forced off [their lands]. And new waves were on the way, new waves of the dispossessed and the homeless, hardened, intent, and dangerous.

John Steinbeck, The Grapes of Wrath. New York: Viking Press, 1939, pp. 317–18.

writer Carey McWilliams, himself an Oakie child in the 1930s, later remembered.

> They were [supposedly] shiftless and lazy and irresponsible and had too many children. . . . Once I went into the foyer of this third-rate [movie theater] in Bakersfield [California] and I saw a sign [that read] "Negroes and Oakies upstairs."[79]

The plight of the Oakies was burned into America's cultural consciousness by John Steinbeck's 1939 novel, *The Grapes of Wrath,* and by the movie version made shortly afterwards. Both showed how poor migrant workers experienced intense poverty and prejudice in the Depression years. To their surprise and sadness, they found themselves among the minority groups that frequently suffered more that the rest of the country during the worst economic downturn in modern times.

Epilogue

The Depression's End and its Legacy

In 1936, as that year's presidential election approached, the impression remained strong among a majority of Americans that the New Deal was making a dent in the Depression. True, no solid facts and figures showed that the economic slump would end soon, and unemployment remained high (though at 17 percent it was eight points lower than it had been at the Depression's height, in 1933). But there was a general feeling that Roosevelt and his New Dealers were doing everything humanly possible to turn things around. So Roosevelt won the election. In a landslide, he defeated his Republican opponent, Kansas governor, Alf Landon, who managed to win only two of the forty-eight states (Maine and Vermont).

Roosevelt won an unprecedented third term in 1940, this time beating Republican Wendell Willkie. At this juncture, the New Deal was beginning to wind down. And though its programs

had indeed alleviated much suffering in the country, they had not ended the national crisis. In 1940, more than a decade after the Depression had begun, the unemployment rate was still a crippling and unacceptable 14.6 percent.

The Ultimate Public Works Project

Moreover, that three-point drop in unemployment since 1936 was due less to FDR's programs and more to an upsurge in war production. World War II had begun in Europe in 1939. Though the United States was not yet directly involved, it began supplying Britain and other allies with large amounts of military equipment. This trend increased, creating many new jobs in the process. By 1941, the level of industrial production in the United States was 30 percent higher than it had been early in 1929, before the stock market crash. And American industrial output soared still higher after the Japanese attack on Pearl Harbor, in December 1941, which plunged the United States fully into the ongoing world war. In this way, the Great Depression ended at last. "In the final analysis," John Chalberg remarks, "the American defense industry proved to be the ultimate public works project."[80]

Under these circumstances, the question for economists and historians became: how much did the New Deal contribute to the national recovery? Some experts later concluded that Roosevelt's domestic assault on the Depression had been a failure or nearly so. They said that he conducted a large, expensive, and ultimately ineffective experiment. In their view, he and his New Dealers continually failed to balance the federal budget, greatly increased the national debt, and erected a huge, unwieldy bureaucracy. But others were more generous in their analysis of the New Deal. It helped to almost double national income

The interior of Chrysler Corporation's tank arsenal, just one of the factories making military equipment for use in World War II. The upsurge in war production helped to pull the United States out of the Depression.

in its first seven years, they said, and employed millions of jobless, desperate people. Most importantly, Roosevelt and the New Deal restored the country's morale, which had reached an all-time low during the Depression's early years.

Moreover, Roosevelt's defenders pointed out, there was no way to tell what the New Deal might have accomplished had the war not intervened. Joe Marcus, a prominent economist in the 1930s, said, "The war did end the Depression. That doesn't mean that something else might not have ended it."[81] In fact, Marcus and others held that it is possible a few more years of vigorous, costly New Deal programs might have brought the economy back on track. It is true that the government borrowed a lot of the money to fund its New Deal projects, in the process creating a big deficit. Yet in a similar manner, the government borrowed most of the money for its costly war spending, which also created a deficit. The difference, as McElvaine points out, was in the scale of the borrowing and spending:

> The military buildup of 1940–1941 did more to revive American industry and reduce unemployment than had any New Deal program. This is not, though, the reproach of Roosevelt's policies that it may seem. It simply means that the deficit-spending, "demand-side" approach that the New Deal had used timidly was shown to work when employed boldly. Rather than representing a reversal of the

New Deal prescription, the military spending of 1940 and subsequent years represented a much larger dose of the same medicine.[82]

Minimum Levels of Public Welfare

Arguments over the immediate successes or failures of the New Deal aside, there is no doubt that the Depression and New Deal impacted the country in major and lasting ways. "Roosevelt's reforms profoundly altered the United States," as McElvaine puts it, "and their consequences continue to be felt most perceptibly [more than] a half century later."[83]

In the long run, various large-scale social programs, including Social Security, remained in place and became accepted fixtures of American life. Just two decades after the Depression's end, noted American historian Richard Hofstadter pointed out:

> After 1936, not even the Republicans quarreled in their party platforms with such reforms as the Social Security Act, minimum wages and hours, improved housing conditions for low-income families, or the insuring of bank deposits.[84]

Indeed, before the advent of the Depression and the creation of the New Deal to combat it, the United States had no national old-age pension plan, no aid to dependent children, no federal housing, no federal compensation for the

Two children play as their mother applies for Aid for Families with Dependent Children (AFDC), a program created in the Social Security Act of 1935.

unemployed, no federal school lunch program for poor children, no minimum wages, and no government welfare system. Today, even the staunchest political conservatives believe that in a humane society some minimum level of government aid is required to help those citizens who are in dire need. And the New Deal essentially provided the basic ideals and structure of that aid. According to historian Anthony Badger:

The Depression had exhausted private, local, and state resources for relief before 1933. New Deal welfare programs gave the unemployed money and jobs. The lasting loyalty of low-income voters to Roosevelt expressed their appreciation of the very real and essential benefits they received. . . . The New Deal welfare programs provided direct assistance to perhaps as many as 35 percent of the population. It bequeathed [passed on] a commitment to a minimum level of social welfare from which successive governments have never been entirely able to escape.[85]

The New Deal also helped the country's poorest citizens in the long run by eliminating child labor. It also wiped out sweat shops that exploited men, women, and children by grossly underpaying them and forcing them to work in substandard conditions.

Other changes wrought by the Depression and New Deal that are still felt today include many in the economic realm. The 1933 Securities Act made company heads criminally liable for misinformation in their financial statements. The 1934 Securities and Exchange Act provided for government supervision of the stock market, making another crash like the one in 1929 less likely. Also, the 1934 Federal Housing Administration began what is now a time-honored tradition in the mortgage market. Thanks to that New Deal program, which is still in place (as part of the Department of Housing and Urban Development), the government insures construction loans and home mortgages. That allows hundreds of thousands of people each year attain the "American dream" of owning their own home.

Helping People Believe in Themselves

These and other crucial and lasting na-tional benefits that emerged from the Depression era and the New Deal are material in nature. They can be examined over time and analyzed and weighed by looking at statistics, poll results, and economic figures. A less tangible, but no less important, effect that the era had on the country was more psychological in nature. The suffering that millions of Americans endured in the Depression, followed by the enormous collective response embodied by the New Deal, boosted the public's morale at a time when it had reached a dangerously low ebb. In both the short and long run, this in many ways restored Americans' sense of pride in themselves, and reminded them of what they could accomplish if they rose to the challenge. In Hofstadter's words, "The New Deal had taken up a people brought to the brink of despair by poverty and failure and had restored their morale." Even more to the point, the New Deal reinstated the American people's "belief that a democratic people could cope with its own problems in a democratic way."[86]

The ultimate legacy of the Great Depression, therefore, was that it forced a great people who had been humbled by a catastrophe to take stock of their worth and ultimately to rise above and beyond their predicament. In so doing, their nation became economically and militarily the strongest on Earth. And for the remainder of the twentieth century, the United States led the world in industrial output, science and invention, and the spread of freedom and democratic tradi-

A long line of men wait to receive cabbage and potatoes from a government relief agency. The Great Depression and the New Deal led to the United States becoming the strongest military and economic country on Earth.

tions. Thus, America's great Depression-era achievement, expressed first through the New Deal and later through the successful war effort, "was to introduce the United States to the twentieth century," as the late, great historian Arthur M. Schlesinger stated it.

Roosevelt [equipped] the liberal [i.e., Democratic] party with a philosophy of government intervention—a belief, as he put it, that "the government has the definite duty to use all its power and resources to meet the new social problems with new social controls." Much of the New Deal was imperfect, abortive, or ambiguous. . . . But the shortcomings of the New Deal vanish in the general perspective of its supreme success: that is, in the restoration of America as a fighting faith, and in the restoration of democracy as a workable way of life. . . . The New Deal took a broken and despairing land and gave it new confidence in itself.[87]

Notes

Introduction: Trying to Imagine the Unimaginable

1. John C. Chalberg, "Introduction," in William Dudley, ed., *The Great Depression: Opposing Viewpoints.* San Diego: Greenhaven Press, 1994, p. 14.
2. Katharine D. Lumpkin and Dorothy W. Douglas, *Child Workers in America.* New York: Robert M. McBride, 1937, p. 4.
3. Quoted in Studs Terkel, *Hard Times: An Oral History of the Great Depression.* New York: Random House, 2000, p. 45.
4. Quoted in Robert McElvaine, *The Great Depression: America 1929–1941.* New York: Random House, 1993, p. 174.
5. Quoted in Terkel, *Hard Times,* p. 46.
6. Quoted in Dudley, *The Great Depression,* p. 36.
7. Quoted in Howard Zinn, *A People's History of the United States.* New York: HarperCollins, 2005, p. 379.
8. Quoted in McElvaine, *The Great Depression,* p. 175.
9. Quoted in McElvaine, *The Great Depression,* p. 174.
10. McElvaine, *The Great Depression,* p. xiii.

Chapter 1: The Onset of the Great Depression

11. Zinn, *A People's History of the United States,* p. 373.
12. McElvaine, *The Great Depression,* p. 38.
13. Samuel E. Morison, *The Oxford History of the American People.* New York: Oxford University Press, 1965, p. 937.
14. Edward R. Ellis, *A Nation in Torment: The Great Depression, 1929–1939.* New York: Capricorn, 1970, p. 103.
15. Quoted in Terkel, *Hard Times,* p. 424.
16. Quoted in Terkel, *Hard Times,* p. 66.
17. Quoted in Terkel, *Hard Times,* p. 73.
18. Gerald W. Johnston, *Franklin D. Roosevelt: Portrait of a Great Man.* New York: William Morrow, 1967, pp. 119–20.
19. Quoted in Terkel, *Hard Times,* p. 424.
20. Quoted in Terkel, *Hard Times,* p. 425.
21. Quoted in Terkel, *Hard Times,* p. 20.
22. Quoted in Morison, *Oxford History of the American People,* p. 945.

Chapter 2: Hoover's Inadequate Remedies

23. Quoted in Morison, *Oxford History of the American People,* p. 945.
24. T.H. Watkins, *The Great Depression: America in the 1930s.* Boston: Little, Brown and Company, 1993 p. 61.
25. Quoted in White House Biography of Herbert Hoover. http://www.whitehouse.gov/history/presidents/hh31.html
26. Quoted in White House Biography of Herbert Hoover.
27. Herbert Hoover, "Rugged Individualism Speech of October 22, 1928," in Richard Hofstadter, ed., *Great Issues in American History: A Documentary Record, Volume II, 1864–1957.* New York: Vintage, 1960, pp. 338–9.
28. Hoover, "Rugged Individualism Speech," in *Great Issues in American History,* pp. 340–43.
29. Quoted in William S. Myers and Walter H. Newton, *The Hoover Administration: A Documented Narrative.* New York: Scribner's, 1936, pp. 63–64.
30. Quoted in Morison, *Oxford History of the American People,* p. 946.
31. Quoted in Anthony J. Badger, *The New Deal: The Depression Years, 1933–1940.* New York: Farrar, Straus and Giroux, 1989, p. 48.
32. Quoted in William E. Leuchtenburg, ed., *The New Deal: A Documentary History.* New York: Harper and Row, 1968, p. 11.
33. Quoted in McElvaine, *The Great Depression,* p. 52.

Chapter 3: Roosevelt and the Hundred Days

34. Quoted in Dudley, *The Great Depression,* pp. 83–84.
35. Don Nardo, *Franklin D. Roosevelt: U.S. President.* New York: Chelsea House, 1996, pp. 59–60.
36. Franklin D. Roosevelt, "First Inaugural Address," in Richard Hofstadter, ed., *Great Issues in American History: A Documentary Record, Volume II, 1864–1957.* New York: Vintage Books, 1960, pp. 352–7.
37. Quoted in Sharon M. Hanes and Richard C. Hanes, *Great Depression and New Deal: Primary Sources.* Farmington Hills, MI: Gale, 2003, p. 29.
38. Quoted in Franklin D. Roosevelt, *The Public Papers and Addresses of Franklin D. Roosevelt, Volume Two.* New York: Random House, 1938, pp. 62–63.
39. Franklin D. Roosevelt, "Letter of March 13, 1933 to John S. Lawrence," in Elliot Roosevelt, ed., *FDR: His Personal Letters, 1928–1945, Volume One.* New York: Duell, Sloan and Pearce, 1950, pp. 338–9.
40. McElvaine, *The Great Depression,* p. 149.
41. Quoted in Richard Hofstadter et al, *The United States: The History of a Republic.* Englewood Cliffs, NJ: Prentice-Hall, 1957, p. 666.
42. Quoted in Terkel, *Hard Times,* p. 250.

43. Quoted in Morison, *Oxford History of the American People*, p. 959.

Chapter 4: A Grand Experiment: The New Deal

44. Quoted in Terkel, *Hard Times*, pp. 247–8.
45. Quoted in Terkel, *Hard Times*, p. 267.
46. Quoted in Terkel, *Hard Times*, pp. 274–5.
47. Franklin D. Roosevelt, "Presidential Statement Upon Signing the Social Security Act, August 14, 1935" in *The Public Papers and Addresses of Franklin D. Roosevelt, Volume Four.* New York: Random House, 1938, p. 324.
48. Quoted in Dudley, *The Great Depression*, p. 171.
49. Quoted in Arthur M. Schlesinger Jr., *The Coming of the New Deal.* Boston: Houghton Mifflin, 1959, p. 311.
50. Frances Perkins, "The Social Security Act," in Leutchenburg, *The New Deal*, pp. 85–86.
51. McElvaine, *The Great Depression*, pp. 158–9.
2. Quoted in Terkel, *Hard Times*, p. 249.
53. Frances Perkins, *Two Views of American Labor.* Los Angeles: Institute of Industrial Relations, 1965, pp. 10–11.
54. Nardo, *Franklin D. Roosevelt*, p. 74.
55. Franklin D. Roosevelt, "Ninth Fireside Chat," March 9, 1937. http://www.millercenter.virginia.edu/scripps/digitalarchive/speeches/spe_1937_0309_roosevelt
56. Quoted in Leutchenburg, *The New Deal*, p. 214.

Chapter 5: Life and Leisure During the Depression

57. Quoted in Rita Van Amber, *Stories and Recipes of the Great Depression of the 1930s, Volume Two.* Menomone, WI: Van Amber, 1993, pp. 87–88.
58. Quoted in Watkins, *The Great Depression*, p. 125.
59. McElvaine, *The Great Depression*, pp. 172–3.
60. Quoted in McElvaine, *The Great Depression*, p. 172.
61. Quoted in McElvaine, *The Great Depression*, p. 173.
62. Quoted in Dudley, *The Great Depression*, pp. 34–35.
63. Quoted in Badger, *The New Deal*, p. 11.
64. McElvaine, *The Great Depression*, pp. 340–41.
65. Quoted in McElvaine, *The Great Depression*, p. 184.

Chapter 6: Women and Minorities in the Depression

66. Susan Ware, "Women and the New Deal," in Harvard Sitkoff, ed., *Fifty Years Later: The New Deal Evaluated.* New York: Knopf, 1985, pp. 115–16.
67. Quoted in McElvaine, *The Great Depression*, p. 182.
68. Ware, "Women and the New Deal," p. 129.
69. Quoted in McElvaine, *The Great Depression*, p. 187.
70. Edwin P. Hoyt, *The Tempering Years.* New York: Scribner's, 1963, p.117.
71. Harold L. Ickes, "The Negro as a Citizen," in Howard Zinn, ed., *New*

Deal Thought. Indianapolis: Bobbs-Merrill, 1966, p. 341.

72. Quoted in Theodore Rosengarten, *All God's Dangers: The Life of Nate Shaw*. New York: Knopf, 1974, pp. 299–300.

73. Quoted in Raymond Wolters, "The New Deal and the Negro," in John Braeman, ed., *The New Deal: The National Level*. Columbus: Ohio State University Press, 1975, pp. 208–9.

74. Quoted in Ted Morgan, *FDR: A Biography*. New York: Simon and Schuster, 1985, p. 418.

75. Wolters, "The New Deal and the Negro," p. 176.

76. Ickes, "The Negro as a Citizen," p. 343.

77. Quoted in Morison, *Oxford History of the American People*, pp. 983–4.

78. From a 1997 interview with Don Nardo.

79. Quoted in Terkel, *Hard Times*, p. 243.

Epilogue: The Depression's End and its Legacy

80. Quoted in Dudley, *The Great Depression*, p. 121.

81. Quoted in Terkel, *Hard Times*, p. 269.

82. McElvaine, *The Great Depression*, p. 320.

83. McElvaine, *The Great Depression*, p. 307.

84. Hofstadter, *The United States*, p. 675.

85. Badger, *The New Deal*, p. 301.

86. Hofstadter, *The United States*, pp. 674–5.

87. Arthur M. Schlesinger Jr., "The Broad Accomplishments of the New Deal," in Edwin C. Rozwenc, ed., *The New Deal: Revolution or Evolution?* Boston: D.C. Heath, 1968, p.101.

For More Information

Books

William Dudley, ed., *The Great Depression: Opposing Viewpoints.* San Diego: Greenhaven Press, 1994. A fulsome collection of original articles, speeches, and other writings from and about the Depression era.

Mary Gow, *The Stock Market Crash of 1929: Dawn of the Great Depression.* Berkeley Heights, NJ: Enslow, 2003. An informative overview of the key event in the onset of the Great Depression.

Sharon M. Hanes and Richard C. Hanes, *Great Depression and New Deal: Primary Sources.* Farmington Hills, MI: Gale, 2003. A very useful collection of original sources relating to the Great Depression.

William E. Leuchtenburg, ed., *The New Deal: A Documentary History.* New York: Harper and Row, 1968. A hefty collection of articles, speeches, letters, and other original documents from the Depression era, including both pro and con opinions of Roosevelt and his policies.

Richard H. Levey, *Dust Bowl!* New York: Bearport, 2005. A well-written account of the massive loss of farms and displacement of farm families in the American heartland during the Great Depression.

Robert McElvaine, *The Great Depression: America 1929–1941.* New York: Random House, 1993. A reputable scholar delivers one of the best available general overviews of the Great Depression.

Susan Renberger, *A Multicultural Portrait of the Great Depression.* Tarrytown, NY: Marshall Cavendish, 1995. Effectively covers the Great Depression from the often neglected viewpoints of minority groups, many of whom suffered worse than average white Americans during the crisis.

Amity Shlaes, *The Forgotten Man: A New History of the Great Depression.* New York: HarperCollins, 2007. An expert in economics has crafted a thoughtful and revealing look at the Great Depression, emphasizing the courage and hard work of ordinary American citizens during the crisis.

Studs Terkel, *Hard Times: An Oral History of the Great Depression.* New York: Random House, 2000. A widely respected journalist and social commentator presents a large and fascinating collection of remembrances of the Depression era by more than 160 Americans from all walks of life.

Internet

America from the Great Depression to World War II

http://memory.loc.gov/ammem/fsowhome.html

Displays several links to archives of many excellent photos taken during the 1930s.

Dance Marathons

http://www.streetswing.com/histmain/d5marthn.htm

Tells about the dance marathons of the 1930s, including a list of some of the major marathons and several sources for further research.

Discrimination Against Blacks and Poor People in the Depression

http://memory.loc.gov/ammem/ndlpedu/features/timeline/depwwii/race/homework.html

These eyewitness accounts of prejudice are part of an excellent online series about the Depression presented by the U.S. Library of Congress. Follow the links provided to examine other aspects of the crisis.

The Dust Bowl of the 1930s

http://www.ptsi.net/user/museum/dustbowl.html

An easy-to-read and informative overview of the disastrous Dust Bowl, supplemented by contemporary photos of the devastation.

Hollywood in the Thirties

http://www.geocities.com/Hollywood/Lot/4344/index.html

An excellent history of the films of the 1930s, highlighted by numerous photos and drawings.

The Stock Market Crash of 1929

http://www.pbs.org/fmc/timeline/estockmktcrash.htm

PBS presents a short, well-written synopsis of the crash and why it occurred.

Tennessee Valley Authority: Electricity for All

http://newdeal.feri.org/tva/

Tells what the TVA is and why it was established, as well as provides numerous links to sites dealing with various aspects of the TVA in more detail.

Women's Work Relief in the Great Depression

http://mshistory.k12.ms.us/features/feature49/women.htm

An informative overview of some of the attempts to create jobs for women during the Great Depression.

Movies

The Grapes of Wrath (1940) This excellent film version of John Steinbeck's great novel about migrant workers during the Depression benefit's from top-notch acting by Henry Fonda and sturdy direction by John Ford.

They Shoot Horses, Don't They? (1969) Explores the good and bad points of Depression-era dance marathons in dramatic fashion, with a fine performance by Jane Fonda.

Index

speech to/reaction by citizens, 38–40
See also New Deal
Roosevelt, Theodore, 54
"Rugged individualism" speech,
Hoover, 27
Rural families, 61
Russia, Communist takeover, 26

School band concerts, 67
Securities Act (1933), 90
Securities and Exchange Act (1934), 90
Self-help philosophy, of Hoover, 25–27
Shack/shanty dwellings, 9–10, 32
Shady business practices, 16
Shoes shortages, 64
Sitcom shows, on radio, 68
Social Security Act (1935), 50, 51, 52, 75,
89
Soup kitchens, 10–11, 62
Sporting events, 67
Stagecoach movie, 67
Steinbeck, John, 84, 85
Stock market panic/collapse, 13, 18–20
Stockard, George, 61
Suicides, 12, 65
Supreme Court, 58, 60

Tariff lowering strategy, of Hoover, 29
Tennessee Valley Authority (TVA), 45,
46, 50
Terkel, Studs, 78
Tornadoes, 8
Truman, Harry S, 73
Truth-in-Securities Act, 45
Tugwell, Rex, 38, 48

Unemployment
derogatory terms, 64
influence on family roles, 65–67
job creation, 52–55
job hunting, 63–65
post-Black Tuesday, 20, 63

pre-Black Tuesday, 13–14
See also New Deal initiatives

Violence, 66

Walker, Charles, 32
Wall Street, 18–20
Ware, Susan, 73–74
Wayne, John, 67
Wealth, uneven distribution, 14–15
Wealthy Americans, donations for
poor people, 28
Welfare programs, 89–90
Western movies, 67
White, Walter, 79
Willkie, Wendell, 86
Wilson, Woodrow, 26
Women, of Great Depression
difficulties of married women, 74
discrimination against, 74, 76
efforts of Roosevelt, Eleanor, 73–74
second-class citizen status, 76
symbolic gains, 72
Works Progress Administration
(WPA), 44, 55, 58, 74
World War I, 37
Hoover's European food programs,
26
veterans, march on Washington
D.C., 33
World War II
internment of Japanese Americans,
54
Japanese attack on Pearl Harbor, 87
military buildup (1940-1941), 88
onset in Europe, 86
U.S. recovery from, 9

Youngstown, Ohio. *See* Shack/shanty
dwellings

Zinn, Howard, 13–14

Picture Credits

Cover: The Library of Congress

American Stock/Hulton Archive/Getty Images, 32

AP Images, 17, 21, 36, 41, 48, 64, 91

© Bettmann/Corbis, 7, 19, 26, 51, 56, 70, 82, 84, 87

Carl Mydans/Time & Life Pictures/ Getty Images, 54

© Corbis, 6

Courtesy of the FDR Library, 31

© Eudora Welty/Corbis, 80

FPG/Hulton Archive/Getty Images, 18

Gordon Parks/Hulton Archive/Getty Images, 73

Hulton Archive/Getty Images, 29

Keystone/Hulton Archive/Getty Images, 39

Lewis W. Hine/Hulton Archive/Getty Images, 24

Margaret Bourke-White/Time & Life Pictures/Getty Images, 43

MPI/Hulton Archive/Getty Images, 46

National Archives and Records Administration, 33, 57

New York Times Co./Hulton Archive/ Getty Images, 7

Selznick/MGM/The Kobal Collection/ The Picture Desk, Inc., 68

Stephen Ferry/Getty Images, 89

Stock Montage/Hulton Archive/Getty Images, 6

The Library of Congress, 10, 11, 44, 53, 59, 62, 66, 75, 77

Topical Press Agency/Hulton Archive/ Getty Images, 14

About the Author

Historian and award-winning author, Don Nardo, has written many books for young people about American history, including *The Salem Witch Trials, The American Revolution, The Mexican-American War, The Declaration of Independence,* several volumes on the history and culture of Native Americans, and biographies of presidents Thomas Jefferson, Andrew Johnson, and Franklin D. Roosevelt. Mr Nardo lives with his wife Christine in Massachusetts.